BARQUES, SPARKS & SHARKS

Len Wilson

ORKNEYOLOGY
PRESS

Published by Orkneyology Press
Stromness, Orkney Islands
www.orkneyology.com

ISBNs:
978-1-915075-15-4 – paperback
978-1-915075-16-1– ebook

Book sales:
https://shop.orkneyology.com/collections/orkneyology-press-books

Text © 2025 by Len Wilson
All rights reserved.

Illustrations by the author and from family collections or public domain except where indicated

The contents of this book may not be reproduced in any form without written permission from the publishers, except for short extracts for quotations or review.

To my wife and family ~

Lily, Magnus, Laurence
and granddaughter Thea

Contents

	Foreword	i
	Acknowledgements	iii
	All aboard…	v
1	The Captain and the Carpenter	1
2	Sparked into Action	7
3	Port Out, Starboard Home	15
4	Twenty Thousand Leagues	31
5	The Wild West	43
6	Shell Shocks	55
7	White Rabbits, Dark Fears	69
8	Wild Sheep Chase	85
9	Over and Out	93
10	Latter-day Vikings	103
	Appendix: The Fallen	127

*To the gull's way and the whale's way
where the wind's like a whetted knife*
~ John Masefield

Foreword

"The winds are mad," wrote the 17th-century scholar Robert Burton, "and those men are maddest of all that go to sea."

For Len Wilson it was inevitable, growing up in Stromness at the northern entrance of Scapa Flow where the great ships lay in wartime. There was a long seagoing tradition in his family and in the small island of Graemsay where they came from. At the age of six months he was sitting in his grandfather's yole, and by the time he was four he was standing at the tiller of his father's boat.

A natural storyteller, Len crafts a tale as well as he can build a boat (another part of his work experience over the years). With warmth and humour, he takes a sheer delight in the people and places that he encounters along the way.

By the age of 16, he was learning about radio, radar and Morse code, and then comes his first call-up: "We're sending you to join the Orient liner R.M.S. *Orion* as 4th radio officer … a 23,000 ton passenger ship sailing for Australia, New Zealand and across the Pacific to Canada and the States."

And so we enter a bygone world, where each officer takes the head of a table in the first class dining saloon. Len finds himself in cummerbund and dinner jacket, amidst pink gin and fine wine, with caviar ("a disappointment") and anchovies for which he developed a taste: "After all, I was brought up on salt fish." One of the radio officer's duties is to gather and type up reports for an on-board daily newspaper for the passengers, with essential news priorities: "the cricket scores, football results and the stock market, in that order."

Ports of call come and go – Cape Town and Table Mountain, Sydney and Perth, Fiji and Hawaii. For his next ship, Len seeks something different, and is allocated to a tramp steamer carrying cargo for Khorramshahr in Iran. And best of all ... "there wasn't a uniform in sight! The mate wore a battered old trilby with the brim turned down and the Old Man went about in a striped shirt and grey trousers with braces."

The stories flow, the ships sail on – steamers with cargoes for Venezuela and West Africa, tankers with oil for the East, a Greek ship loading coal in Communist Poland for Karachi. In the Nigerian port of Calabar, he sees the grave of the Orcadian nurse Margaret Graham, evoking memories of a former missionary – Harry Mowat – who hails him when he is back home in Stromness.

In just four years, a wonderful array of stories and images unfold – "from the high Arctic to the South Sea Islands and so many places in between." Reading this book is like spending an evening in Len's company and hearing his tales from near and far – so sit back and enjoy the journey!

Howie Firth
April 2025

Acknowledgements

I have to thank Norman Davidson for his contributions and search for newspaper articles; Robert Whitton for the invaluable detail from his website at crwhitton.com; Bryce Wilson, Dennis Davidson, Gregor Lamb, Howie Firth and Joan Maynard for reading my drafts; my late mother and father, Cathie and Isaac, for the stories they told to a child, and to members of the wider family who have unwittingly contributed. A special thank you is due to Magnus Wilson for his editorial and proofreading expertise.

Artwork:
Title page artwork by Laurence Wilson
Chapters 1 to 9 by Thea Wilson
Chapter 10 by Bryce Wilson

All aboard...

I crossed the equator ten times – a quarter of a million miles – before I was 22. The oceans were Britain's major highway for centuries, and I was one of its last 'highwaymen'. Orcadians like me were exposed to the waves from childhood and acquired exceptional boat-handling skills at a very young age.

For centuries, overpopulation drove adventurous youths to seek a living far and wide. Like their Viking forefathers, they roamed the oceans, exploring the remotest parts, making history and spreading (or absorbing) influences as they went. Orkney was not a backwater – lying between the North Sea and the Atlantic Ocean, its harbours were pivotal for shipping since the days of the Norsemen.

Following their lead, I served from 1957–61 on passenger liners, cargo vessels, 'tramp' steamers and even an oil tanker, sailing from the high Arctic to the South Seas and many places in between.

'Tramps' had no fixed route, sniffing around for any cargo along the way – a voyage could last up to two years – but it was still a time of great adventure, before long-distance air travel and container shipping. Britain maintained the largest merchant fleet in the world, though not for much longer. Our generation witnessed the end of an era – we were the last of the Vikings.

Skål!

1. The Captain and the Carpenter

He was 'one of us' – the first British subject laid to rest on the Australian continent on 1st May 1770. He succumbed to tuberculosis, barely 33, in the service of King, country and Captain Cook:

> Forby Sutherland, Seaman, departed this Life and in the A.M. his body
> Was buried ashore at the watering place, which occasioned me calling the
> south point of this bay after his name.

Forby Sutherland's memorial stone at Botany Bay

Gotten in fornication

Forbes, or Forby, had come a long way. Sutherland Point, near Botany Bay, is now a favourite spot for diving, but he was originally from the island of Flotta, hidden in Scapa Flow, the deep natural harbour of the Orkney Islands, just beyond the northern tip of Scotland.

My Sutherland granny's family had their roots firmly in the same flat little isle, so it is very likely that Forby was a relative. His baptismal record states bluntly that he was "gotten in fornication" though it is likely that his parents married before the birth. But if his beginning was commonplace, he was destined to join one of the most famous voyages in history, one of a bold generation of sea-faring pioneers who would map the world.

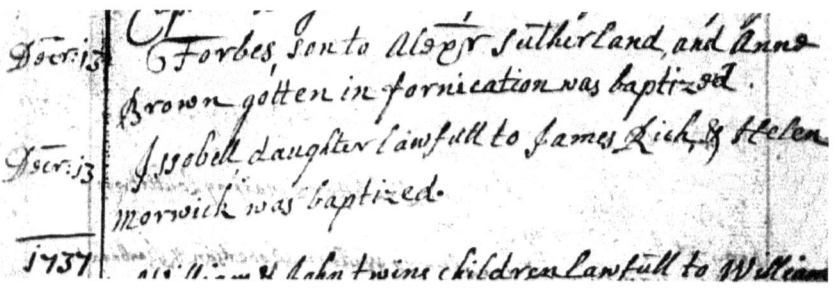

The detail of Forbes Sutherland's baptism in Stromness parish records, 13th December 1736

Like Fair Isle knitting

A generation later (c. 1830), our branch of the Sutherland family moved a much shorter distance to establish their home in Graemsay, an even smaller island squeezed between two violent tidal streams that separate the 'whale's hump' of Hoy from the town of Stromness in Orkney's West Mainland.

Scapa Flow showing Flotta and Graemsay

Living on a tiny speck like Graemsay, about 2 miles by 1 mile, all the families were interlinked like a piece of Fair Isle knitting, often several times through the generations. There was a continuous trickle of new blood into the community, but as soon as one of them took a spouse, they found themselves tied to all the others. It was in this context that the relatively new incomers, Sutherlands and Wilsons, connected to the Graemsay families, including my mother's paternal side, the long-established Ritch, Sinclair and Lyon families.

Icons

While Forby mapped the world, his descendants built it. From 1928 to its completion in 1932, Australia's national bridge, for instance, was made from girders transported by my father and his seafaring colleagues. During Isaac's 12 years as a ship's carpenter with the Port Line, he made 25 circumnavigations running to Australia and New Zealand by various routes, either the Suez or Panama canals or round the Cape of Good Hope, returning via Cape Horn. The iconic Sydney Bridge's prefabricated steel components were all carried out on the Port boats from Newcastle, England.

M.V. *Port Dunedin* passing under Sydney Bridge

Yet, his most notable cargo of all was when Isaac and his *Port Dunedin* shipmates transported Captain Cook's Yorkshire cottage, stone by historic stone, stuffed into umpteen packing cases, in order to be rebuilt for Melbourne's centenary in 1934. Poor Forby would have blinked in bewilderment.

The Captain and the Carpenter

Isaac displaying his handiwork on board *Port Fremantle,* and going ashore in Buenos Aires

This was already heroic history by the time I was born. But it was impossible to ignore Dad's past and the past of almost every other male relative that preceded him. At a very early age, I learned to count to ten in Spanish while our home, like so many in Stromness, displayed a child-tempting collection of artefacts, treasure, booty and plunder along with all those mysterious sepia-tinted photos from every end of the earth.

To paint a picture of what life was like for so many Orkney families, shaped by the violent tidal streams of poverty and the quest for wealth, I've taken a look at two centuries of my own extended relatives' seafaring experience – the triumphs, tragedies and all in-between – starting with my own escapades among barques, 'sparks' and sharks, in chapters to come.

2. Sparked into Action

The author with his grand-uncle
Captain Charlie Ritch, 1940

Mr. Hitler woke me – at least the thump of our coastal defences did. Soldiers regularly paraded in front of our home at 15 Well Park while army lorries passed all day. Boys would cling to the back of them with their feet off the ground to get a free lift through town. War was fun, for some.

I was born in Stromness, November 1938 – our front door just 25 yards above the rocky beach at Ness. It was certainly more than a stone's throw from the major seats of power (Downing Street,

The White House or the *Führerbunker*) but it was still the northern entrance to Scapa Flow, the home of the British Naval Fleet and the most heavily fortified part of Britain during World War II.

Busy as Piccadilly

With an army camp beside us and an armed sentry on the gate, we listened for the morning bugle-call: 'Come to the cookhouse door boys, come to the cookhouse door.' The gun battery was close-by too, with its resounding boom. Two fast boats towed floating targets in Hoy Sound for the gunners to lob shells at them.

The whole place throbbed as busy as Piccadilly Circus on a mad Saturday before Christmas. Naval launches ran back and fore as steam puffers delivered stores for the armed forces – all manner of cargo vessels and water carriers constantly supplied the fleet as it belched oily vapours into a sky buzzing with aircraft, low across the water, like dragonflies. I can still recall a seaplane being towed in and anchored at the north end of the harbour where it somehow sank later that day. War was a spectacle.

My father had already 'swallowed the anchor' in 1937 after a million miles of sea-travel. Now he was building army camps while serving in the Home Guard with a rifle behind our kitchen door and bullets on the mantelpiece. Later, when Italian prisoners arrived in Orkney, we'd regularly spot one in the street. Their green uniform had a diamond-shaped 'target' in the middle of their back. "Green cabbages!" we yelled, till they gave chase. War was a bit of a lark.

Our lads were good to the children. We attended film shows at the Garrison Theatre: *Gone with the Wind* and *Buffalo Bill*. They gave us a Christmas party at the camp and sent coconuts to the school. When Gracie Fields, star of screen and stage, was in Scapa Flow entertaining servicemen, she visited Well Park to brighten the day for the mothers and children. She chatted and tickled my chin as I flashed a toothless gurgle – or so my mother told me.

When victory eventually came, a fancy dress parade cavorted through the street. But the fun was still not over. Every family benefited in some way from the proliferation of surplus equipment that was dispersed, some of it free, with the rest at bargain sales or by auction. Our parents bought an army camp, whilst my brother Bryce and I were thrilled by the khaki canvas bags for our school books. We could now march smartly along the street into the broad, sunlit uplands.

Waves are my teachers

I enjoyed school but was often distracted. History, geography and maths were interesting but uninspiring. Science commanded my attention and I did excel at technical subjects. But I was at my best on the sea. My grandfathers, uncles and my father all had boats. I had made my first of countless crossings of Hoy Sound when six months old. By the age of four, I was standing proud at the tiller of my father's boat. I decided there and then that I would be a sailor. The waves would be my teachers, the tides my professors.

Fishing was the core curriculum: setting creels for lobster and partans (crab), and trolling for lythe (pollack). Going 'oot west' for cod and haddock wasn't so popular as it was usually accompanied by sea-sickness – a painful issue we will bring up later. But the most exciting catch was at the mackerel for they were voracious feeders which we hauled in six at a time. Or so it seemed.

My seafaring elders tut-tutted, twisting their waxed moustaches as the tide pulled me in their wake. They knew the risks and hardships in their every creaking bone. Eventually, Uncle Charlie, a master mariner himself, suggested the wisest course: "If you must go to sea, go as a radio officer. That way you'll easily get a shore job when you're ready for it." A spark had ignited in my mind, charting the way ahead.

Logarithms in Leith

Mr. Fisher, the principal, took me aside at interview, suggesting I get qualified ahead of my 18th birthday to avoid compulsory National Service – the dreaded draft. So that was it. Barely out of short trousers, I left school at 16 for Leith Nautical College.

My lecturers were ancient mariners. Harry *"When I was in the Ark"* Watson liked to tell us how he survived a munitions ship explosion in Canada: "I was out walking four miles away and it blew my hat off." Meanwhile, Andrew Bogie, the department head, was a radar theory and maintenance man to his finger-tips. No calculators and computers in those days – he taught us to calculate logarithms without looking up any tedious tables, a practice I put to good use when I forgot to bring them to a maths examination.

The staff of Leith Nautical College beside T.S. *Dolphin* c. 1960.
Second row: 2nd left Ted Whitehead. Front row: 1st left Fred Boettcher,
3rd Mr. Fisher, 4th Andrew Bogie and, far right of picture, Harry Watson.
(Edinburgh College)

Bright Sparks

Learning Morse code is a bit like reading Braille while juggling on a unicycle, but I had to master it – *pronto*. I needed a speed of 20 words per minute to get my radio officer's 2nd class certificate. (1st class is a zippy 25 w.p.m., with a higher level in radio theory, but that could wait.) Radar maintenance was a very useful add-on, with an examination on the theory and a practical test.

No satellite communication in those days, of course. Even *Sputnik* was barely off the launchpad. Ships relied on radio. Early Marconi equipment had used a spark transmitter generating a loud and brilliant discharge between two dome-shaped electrodes. It was all a bit Frankensteinian, hence the operator's nickname, 'Sparks'. On large passenger liners, we had 24-hour coverage, but most of the ships I sailed on carried only one radio officer covering 8 hours a day (two hours on, two hours off). Off-watch periods were monitored by an auto-alarm receiver which rang a bell on receipt of a distress signal. Usually, the bleary-eyed 'Sparks' found his sleep rudely interrupted by yet another false alarm.

Still, we were wizards of the waves. When the strength of medium wave radio signals petered out beyond 300 miles, we had to figure out how the layers of the ionosphere vary in strength and altitude in order to use short wave for longer distances. It required a good understanding and a degree of art to get our techno-magic to work.

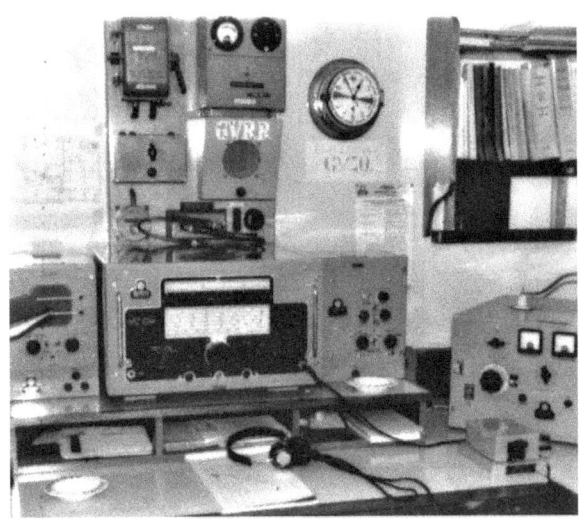

The radio desk on M.V. *Kumba*.

Left to right: Standby receiver, main receiver, auto-key device and the emergency transmitter. The clock kept on GMT.

Unsinkable

Despite winds of change, Britain ruled the radio waves. Having Commonwealth countries made our communications much more efficient. The names of radio stations evoked Phileas Fogg in *Around the World in Eighty Days:* the Atlantic was covered by Portishead near Bristol, Halifax in Nova Scotia and Cape Town. Then we had Aden, Bombay, Colombo, Perth, Sydney, Wellington, Hong Kong and Vancouver plus intermediary stations, each cutting the distances we had to cover and sharing out the huge amount of radio traffic that the British fleet generated.

Naturally, the Spaghetti-junction of the seas lay in the English Channel and North Sea, with a continuous clamour of overlapping Morse signals, so it took an expert ear to pick out the message you wanted. By contrast, in the middle of the Pacific you might hardly hear a signal for days on end.

Either way, there wasn't much room for idle chit-chat when monitoring the airwaves and logging calls heard. A three minute silence was kept every half hour so that any faint distress signals might be heard, while some ships exchanged daily noon positions so that, in an emergency, there would be a record of their last position. No one forgot how *Titanic* was 'unsinkable'. But with art and skill, 'Sparks' would keep us safe.

The author

Sparked into Action

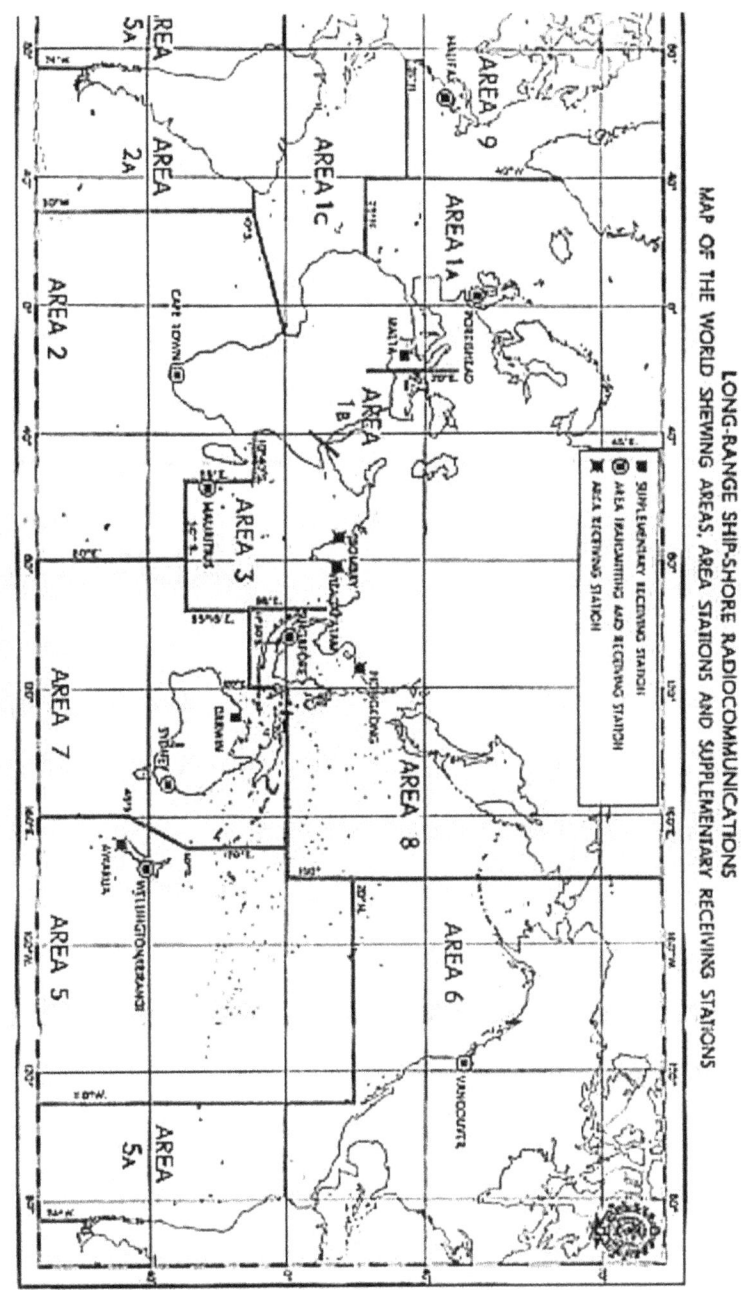

3. Port Out, Starboard Home

R.M.S. *Orion*. Radio callsign GYKL
Built by Vickers Armstrong, Barrow-in-Furness, in 1935. 23,372 g.r.t.
(John Oxley Library, State Library of Queensland)

I stood looking up at the massive ship: "Weel, ah'll no be sick on this een." The *Orion* – pride of the Orient Line – seemed sleeker than an Art Deco cinema and a hell of a lot larger. Marconi International Marine Communication Company (MIMCo) had promised me a job once I got my certificate in 1956, and they certainly kept their word. This was a 23,000 ton liner bound for Australia, New Zealand and across the Pacific to Canada and the States – circumnavigating the known world.

As *Orion* was a passenger vessel, I required a lot of extra uniform. Miller Rayner, Naval Outfitters in Tilbury, made sure I had all the right kit: white shirts (three of each, long sleeved and short sleeved), epaulettes, white collars, black bow tie, black cummerbund, three suits of 'number tens' (long white trousers and jacket buttoned to the neck) plus white footwear. I would not have looked out of place if I'd been page boy to the King of Siam. I even had to pay it all back by monthly instalment from my £28 per month salary, then cart the whole lot home at the end of the trip. And it was never worn again!

Things started to 'hot-up' as sailing day approached, with the crew as busy as termites, ready to sail with about 1,200 passengers on board. We carried about 500 1st class passengers and a larger number of tourist class, mostly emigrants on £10 assisted passages sponsored by the Australian government – about a week's wages for a tradesman.

Our departure was an event in itself. Over a thousand passengers jostled on deck, each clutching the roll of coloured paper streamer they'd thrown ashore for their friends and relatives. The delicate tethers snapped, one by one, as the ship moved out from the dock, embarking upon our epic voyage. For many, it was their last physical contact – sometimes the last ever sighting – of everything they held dear, long before cheap phone calls or easy air travel. We left to an operatic chorus of waved goodbyes and wiping of eyes.

SOS x 2

The ship was like a small town with 460 crew toiling to make sure all were fed, watered and entertained while being kept up to date with a daily news bulletin. We had a hairdresser, beauty parlour, child's nursery, surgery, operating theatre – just in case – plus a swimming pool, deck games and even a small orchestra.

I was allocated the 4 to 8 watch and shared it with the chief radio officer for about a week to acquaint myself with the operating procedures. No sooner had we left the Thames estuary, I got my first experience of an SOS. A vessel was in danger of sinking near the Dutch coast so we kept silent and monitored the situation till help arrived. Little did I realise, my own personal SOS was about to begin:

> Sometimes the ship pitched and sometimes she rolled and sometimes she stood quite still and shivered all over, poised above an abyss of dark water; then she would go swooping down like a scenic railway train into a windless hollow and up again with a rush ... sometimes she would burrow her path, with convulsive nosings and scramblings like a terrier in a rabbit hole; and sometimes she would drop dead like a lift. It was this last movement that caused the most havoc among the passengers. (Evelyn Waugh, *Vile Bodies*)

I started to be sick. I was not excused duty and had to carry a humiliating pail on watch. By day three, I was a staggering zombie, my guts at war with my throat. A lifetime passed till we docked in Las Palmas on day four. It felt like day 44. But I had survived. Just!

R.M.S. *Orion* in Las Palmas

As we left the Canaries, I was starting to get the hang of things, sending a weather observation (or OBS) on every watch and exchanging messages on short wave with Portishead Radio. At night, we copied press reports for an on-board daily newspaper. I had to jot it down by hand and then type onto a stencil sheet for the purser's office to print out on their Gestetner duplicating machine. Historians may note, even if the Prime Minister had resigned or Soviet tanks were on the move, it was impressed upon me that there were three reports I must not miss – the cricket scores, football results and the stock market, in that order.

The crew were old salts. Sid Jones, second radio officer (R/O), was our on-board 'Speedy Gonzalez'. When copying press reports from Bolinas Radio (near San Francisco) at a zippy 28 words per minute, he would stop to light a fag and then catch up effortlessly. It didn't always go according to plan though. OBS weather reports were written in five-digit numerical code words. Sid rattled off the incoming message on the typewriter and passed it up to the bridge above. It came back down almost immediately. He had omitted to depress the numbers key on the typewriter: the forecast was apparently '^&)+% !-"/% £%(&!'.

It's amazing we could type at all. By now, I had my sea-legs, but the ship's heavy, pronounced roll would turn you into a Chaplinesque clown unless you showed some acrobatic flair. Climbing the stairs to my cabin was like a drunken struggle if the ship was rising. You had to hold on, wait for the fall and then nip up effortlessly as a ballerina. Meanwhile, the dining saloon was on 'G' deck with the lowest row of portholes. They regularly dipped below the water as we rolled along, causing a flood when a porthole had not been adequately secured. Cook's buffet was a washout!

Monkey business

Another source of nausea was the shipboard etiquette. It had us dancing like an organ-grinder's monkey at a fancy dress ball. Each officer took the head of a table in the 1st Class dining saloon. Whenever a woman approached, all the men stood until she was seated – as if the Dowager Empress had swept in. Regular blue uniform was worn to breakfast and lunch, with the addition of a black bow tie to dinner. In the tropics, it was 'number tens' for daytime meals. At dinner, navy trousers and black shoes, black cummerbund, white monkey-jacket with epaulettes and black bow tie. No choice: you had to comply.

If the etiquette was a chore, the menu was an eye-popper, bursting with things I'd never seen before and some I'd never heard of. At the captain's welcome party, there was pink gin, fine wine and nibbles with caviare. An acquired taste, the black stuff made cod roe seem like a real delicacy. But it was undoubtedly posh, and that's what mattered. The large tray of appetisers at lunchtime included anchovies that I did develop a taste for as I was brought up on salt fish. Dinner, meanwhile, was a five course affair. There was always a fish entrée and the main might include venison or other exotic meat dishes. We had a variety of up-market desserts that included avocados and whole pineapples that – amazingly for 1957 – did not come from a tin! We picked up fruit from the southern hemisphere as the trip progressed, including paw-paw, passion fruit, kiwi fruit, etc. There were wine waiters whose main task was to top up the water glasses. *Vino* was not in huge demand as we Brits were not yet a wine-drinking nation. Coffee was served in the forward lounge where there was evening entertainment – dancing to the orchestra, or a night of tombola (bingo) while some played cards or chess with a few glasses of pink gin or a fancy cocktail. As the band played on, we hiccupped through the tropics like Jeeves and Wooster.

Down Under

The best perk for a radio officer was freedom from duty whilst in port, which I took full advantage of when we arrived in Cape Town (South Africa). From the top of Table Mountain, the vantage point was dizzying – as much for what I didn't see, as what I did. Looking back, it was still extraordinarily easy to remain blind to the lack of freedom afforded to blacks, whose daily lives were ground down to a permanent underclass after the introduction of the *apartheid* system of segregation ten years earlier. Walking the city streets, I was certainly ignorant about it – but learning. As I returned to the ship later that day, I was befriended by a young African, walking together down through the dock area until we parted company when I boarded the ship. Two days out, a stowaway was discovered in one of our lifeboats. It must have been *him* – I was his 'passport' through the docks, offering a 'perk' which he took full advantage of when he arrived at the ship. The poor fellow's dash for freedom would end with a 'free' passage back to Cape Town on the first available ship.

Cape Town and Table Mountain in 1957

From the Cape to Fremantle (Australia), *Orion* rolled more than ever. The weather was beautifully calm but there was a relentless long and heavy swell coming down from the Indian Ocean when an escort of dolphins joined us, overtaking with playful ease at 18 knots.

My first glimpse of Australia was dazzling, like having a cataract removed. I took a train the short distance to Perth where everything was breathtakingly colourful, sparkling clean and bedecked with exotic plants and flowers – quite unlike the drab, ash-grey, and none too clean post-war Britain I had left behind. No wonder the £10 emigrants were tempted.

In port, all was shipshape on *Orion* for a routine lifeboat drill when a splash turned everyone's heads. The echo bounced across the dock as our motor boat plunged head-first. The forward tackle had snapped, leaving the vessel suspended by the stern and its radio equipment submerged. Luckily, nobody was injured but now we were stuck. New batteries would be needed and everything dried out and laboriously tested.

Nobody likes a delay: not the captain, not the crew and especially not the fretting passengers. I found myself in the thick of it, relaying scores of messages ahead to Adelaide, to advise passengers' friends of the hold up. No one expects lavish praise and I didn't receive any, but working well under pressure was quietly noticed. Once we were under way, *aurora australis* (the Southern Lights) lit up the antipodean sky with a magical swish of dancing technicolour. It felt like nature's pat on the back.

After Adelaide, it was on to Melbourne. (Mother's cousin, Donald Sutherland, came down to meet the 'killer' ship – its propeller had gruesomely sliced open the belly of a whale, he told me, when he'd been a passenger on board.) Though Australia might be an offshoot of the 'green and pleasant' mother country, it still had its own sharp profile. The countryside around Melbourne was impressively itself, with distinctive eucalyptus trees in every direction and dusty red roads stretching to the impossible horizon.

Orion & P&O's *Strathnaver* at Williamstown, Melbourne

The first stage of the trip ended in Sydney where we berthed at The Rocks, the city's historic centre. We had sailed more than 11,000 miles in 30-odd days on what was my first professional voyage. It was only fitting that I took a special interest in 'The Coathanger' – the shapely magnificence of Sydney Bridge – especially as my father had helped ship the steel to build it. Most of the remaining passengers disembarked here, except for the New Zealand contingent.

The Sydney skyline in 1957

Our catering staff fussed about, preparing for a new complement of passengers for the North American run. All the accommodation had to be spotless for their arrival and the menu Americanised. Details mattered. Even names were changed. porridge became rolled oats or, curiously, Uncle Toby's Oats (a local Aussie brand).

Sydney Bridge through the mist

After Sydney (and a day in Auckland) we set course for Suva (Fiji), joined *en route* by a couple of albatrosses, searching for scraps or perhaps just curious. They must have slept on the wing, gliding close alongside the ship to get the benefit of a free ride as our slipstream

Passing Three Kings Islands at the northern tip of New Zealand

carried them forward. Then they'd peel off and quickly rejoin us at the stern, repeating the performance for days on end with hardly a flap of their legendary wings. It was a lesson in perpetual motion.

Circling sharks greeted us with languid menace at the quayside in Suva. A traffic policeman posed for my camera in town, splendidly dressed in his navy shirt and white pencil skirt with its distinct, saw-toothed hemline – ripped clean, as if by Jaws.

Traffic control in Suva

I would later come face-to-face with staunchly traditional Fiji, (see Chapter 6) but meanwhile, another lifeboat drill was needed to practise using the free-hanging rope ladder – surely nothing would go wrong this time. Of course, a ladder hanging loose is impossible to climb in the conventional fashion, but there is a correct procedure – ascending hand over hand on the edge (like climbing a rope) with your heels on the wooden rungs, one foot on each side of the ladder. Our athletic young purser was about 20 feet up – making the captain, crew and country proud – when he caught his trousers on the corner of a rung. It ripped his fly open from top to bottom. No time to hesitate! He rocketed straight to the top as the passengers cheered in delight, reddening his youthful cheeks.

Full steam to Honolulu, we took time to circle – like curious albatrosses – tight round the unfathomably remote Canton Atoll, in order to give passengers a view of the fragile, ring-shaped, coral reef.

Its first inhabitants were, improbably, two British radio operators stationed there in 1937. The perfect scenario for a desert island murder or suicide, or both!

But life at sea prepares you for anything – a passenger with severe appendicitis, for instance. Our young on-board doctor would have to scrub up, but with *Orion's* notorious roll, even the steadiest hand would surely slice and slash – like a propeller ripping the guts of a whale. Teamwork was required. The captain ordered a turn into the swell, dropping the speed to 3 knots with a slow but predictable pitch. We waited … and waited till our cool-headed hero eventually emerged. No burial at sea was required!

In the pink

Waikiki with the Royal Hawaiian Hotel in the background

Hawaii had an exotic reputation as an idyllic, if sometimes garish, place with floral *leis*, grass skirts and historic associations with Captain Cook, even if Honolulu itself had the thoroughly modern appearance of a prosperous American city. I walked the several miles out to the legendary Waikiki Beach, an absolute must-see destination for well-heeled tourists. Native Hawaiians operated a lucrative business to relieve them of their extra cash, taking holidaymakers out in large outrigger canoes to surf back in through large breakers. I couldn't resist the temptation to view the interior of the world-famous Royal Hawaiian Hotel, frequented by the likes of President Roosevelt and Shirley Temple, otherwise known as 'The Pink Palace of the Pacific'. I can duly confirm, it was pink and definitely palatial.

We reached our most northerly Pacific port at Vancouver, British Columbia, in redwood country. Mother's cousin, Brenda Linklater, drove me round on a tour to view the native Totem poles carved with brightly painted faces of mythical beasts and birds in honour of legendary ancestral lineages. In fact, her own lineage intertwined with mine as her Canadian husband, Walter Simmonds, had served in Orkney during World War II, seconded to the RAF as a radar engineer, while their daughter, Sheila, was actually born in our house in Stromness. Yet, even though we had some pretty sturdy wooden clothes poles, we had nothing as totemic as this!

From Vancouver it was a relatively short coastal trip and through the 'Golden Gate' to San Francisco. Parts of it could have been Hong Kong or Shanghai with its Chinese architecture, lanterns and décor. Souvenir shops overflowed with intricate Oriental craft-work, jade sculptures and delicately inlaid boxes with a complicated, secret opening procedure, just like Chairman Mao's China itself. Little did we realise, Chinatown would be a sign of things to come for a future manufacturing superpower.

Yet, all too soon, we were off again with a new compliment of passengers that included a group of youthful Mormon missionaries bound for Fiji, travelling first class, if you don't mind. No booze and not even tea, they still knew how to enjoy themselves, singing popular songs to their own guitar accompaniment.

A point of clarity

The summit of Mt. Wellington, Tasmania

We all had our own missions. On the homeward journey, Hobart was our extra port of call. I joined a group of passengers on Mount Wellington, towering 4,000 feet at the snow-patched summit. We gazed upon 19th century convict settlements with their grim stone walls built on the hillside for no other purpose than to provide hard labour. It was odd to think the men's guilt-induced sweat eventually built and supported a lifestyle – in some cases, a posh lifestyle – that the *Orion* rigorously adhered to as it traversed the oceans with hundreds of £10 hopefuls still searching for the 'good' life. From our chilly vantage point, the perpetual curiosity of the albatross (and the razor-toothed instincts of the shark), had led us all to this point of clarity.

Oddly, *Orion* itself would become a convict ship. Liners always had a problem with cutlery going astray, especially as it made – to put it delicately – an attractive 'souvenir' of the voyage. In order to reduce the losses, the chief steward was paid a 'cutlery bonus' at the end of the trip which was reduced according to the amount that went missing. After a lengthy voyage, the chief and his deputy's petty rivalries had come to boiling point, turning the atmosphere distinctly sour. But revenge is the sweetest form of nectar: the second steward started to dump large quantities of silver-plated forks, serving spoons, ladles and, for all I know, tea caddies and tweezers out through his porthole and into the Indian Ocean. Who can tell how much treasure lies on the bottom, but the culprit himself was caught red-handed and spent the rest of the trip locked in the brig.

After nearly 40,000 miles, and uncountable knives and forks, we finally approached the Portuguese coast. By this point, I had surely passed my apprenticeship. At least, no more sick buckets were needed on watch. I was able to reflect on the voyage and realise what an invaluable experience it had been. It would stand me in good stead for the rest of my life, but I was wearying. I'd reached my own point of clarity. All this formality made me feel like a prisoner. I was looking for *real* adventure. When my chief invited me back next trip I declined politely: "I'll be looking for a tramp steamer next trip." His eyebrows leapt like he'd seen a lunatic, but this was my new mission.

My posh life was almost, but not quite, over. On arrival in Tilbury, I called home. Mother told me, "Aunty Elsie and the boys are in London staying at the Savoy." The good news was, Uncle Charlie worked for the Iraqi Port Authority as a berthing master for Abadan and en route, his employer ensured that his family were well catered for in the very best hotels. And what could be better than The Savoy Hotel? I gave Elsie a call and soon found myself dining on London's finest, frequented by everyone from Winston Churchill to Charlie Chaplin – and all at King Faisal's expense. Little did we know how it would end, but we'll come back to that later (see Chapter 4).

The last rites

My last duty for the Orient Line was, perhaps appropriately, as assistant funeral director, when I was invited to guide a vessel to her graveyard on the Clyde. At 32 years old, she'd seen illustrious service both in peace and war, landing troops in Sicily and at Salerno in the Italian campaign of World War II. "*Otranto* is going round to be scrapped," I was told. "You can join her as second radio officer as you head for home."

R.M.S. *Otranto*. Radio callsign GFKV
Built by Vickers Armstrong, Barrow-in-Furness in 1925. 20,032 g.r.t.
(Allan C Green. The State Library of Victoria)

As we docked, our grand, ocean-going 'barque' ended her journey with her freshly promoted 'sparks', only to be pitilessly scavenged by a circling pack of shamelessly ravenous sharks – the crew. We hungrily set about finding souvenirs. Cutlery was for wimps. Some of us were already helping to unbolt the ship's wheel when – silently and unannounced – the senior Director of the Orient Line appeared to inspect the bridge. Time itself stood still. A dozen eyes darted around before our chief officer managed to blurt something out: "Just removing the wheel to present it to you, sir." A knowing glance from the old director revealed the wisdom of his age: "No lads, you have it for yourselves." The third mate won the draw and I settled for the bell from one of the bridge telephones which rings as our doorbell to this day.

I nabbed another little trophy too. In a Hitchcockian coincidence, the third mate was dashing off to join *Orion* as junior third officer when he left his pipe behind. I slipped it into my pocket, but was too late to catch him ... more on this story later.

Still barely an adult, I was already laden with first class booty and an invaluable treasure of experiences. But I knew it was time for me to leave this poshness behind and become a tramp.

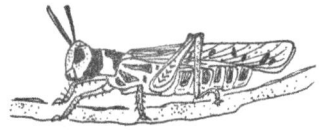

4. Twenty Thousand Leagues

It must have seemed odd to an observer – a half a dozen men sitting reading magazines when suddenly there's a burst of dots and dashes from a loudspeaker in the corner and one lad picks up his bag, leaves the room, heading for the front desk where he will learn his fate. In my case: "We're sending you to join the *Marsdale* in Salford. You'll catch a train here for Manchester and get a taxi down to the docks." This was the cloak-and-dagger, MI6-style procedure in Marconi's Depot in Liverpool, where I now found myself after a brief, three-day trip from the Clyde with the Larrinaga Line.

S.S. *Marsdale*. Radio callsign GBKB
Clyde built for Kaye & Co., 1940. 4980 g.r.t.
(Malcolm Cranfield collection)

Not a uniform in sight

If my ships were getting smaller, my world was expanding. Barely a fifth the size of the *Orion*, the S.S. *Marsdale* was crewed by all-comers. The Old Man, Captain Ferguson, was from Belfast while the first mate was a former Captain Nicholson, originally from Shetland: "I wis retired fur three year," he admitted, "but couldna stan' it, an' ah'm back here as mate." So, we were a dual-monarchy, joined by 'clown prince' Ernie Fernandez as second mate, who despite the name, was actually from Goa (Portugal's Indian colony). More on his pranks later. Nearer to home, our third mate, Austen, hailed from St. Leonard's-on-Sea and our apprentice, Edwards, from Liverpool, was simply known as 'Scouse'. Below deck was even more cosmopolitan, including an actual Indian second engineer (with a BSc degree), plus a couple of lads from behind the Iron Curtain (our Polish third engineer and the carpenter, officially a Latvian 'displaced person' after the Russian occupation of his homeland in World War II). Oiling away in the engine room, the greasers were Arab Lascars from the Yemen, while the other person of note was a Glaswegian able seaman called Flanagan, who had recently served as a 'guest' of Her Majesty for GBH – Grievous Bodily Harm. Obviously, someone to keep an eye on.

My cell on board would surely have interested Amnesty International on humanitarian grounds. Unlike *Orion*, the radio cabin (just behind the chart-room) was so cramped there was only space for the equipment, a chair and maybe one person standing. My personal quarters were hardly any bigger, but the Old Man offered me the pilot's accommodation, five times the size – a welcome upgrade. Better still, we were headed for Khorramshahr in Iran, 65 miles up the Shatt al-Arab and just 15 miles from Abadan where my recent swanky Savoy dining partners, Aunty Elsie and the boys, were spending their summer holiday with their dad. Time to whistle: 'We'll meet again some sunny day'. Egg-fryingly sunny.

It all made for a buoyant mood. Small crowds waved, as if to celebrate, as we passed through the Manchester ship canal. By the time we entered the Irish Sea, I was already enjoying the job. The best thing about it – not a uniform in sight! The mate wore a battered old trilby with the brim turned down, and the Old Man went about in a striped shirt and grey trousers with braces. No 'yessir-no-sir', monkey-grinder antics here.

This was real seafaring. I was learning my trade beyond my duties, often keeping lookout on the bridge with the third mate, chart-plotting and even taking the wheel when the helmsman went down to make us a cup of tea at night. One of my daily tasks was to get a radio time signal to check the ship's chronometer. With the Orient Line there was a bell-push to pass the signal to the chart-room, but on this ship, at the final *beep* I hit the bulkhead with a hammer! Crude but just as effective. Meanwhile, I honed my radio direction-finding, plotting our position as we moved down the Portuguese coast. It was hazardous at night as the sardine boats were out en-masse, displaying only a faint glimmer from their mast-heads. I practised a bit of old fashioned signalling using our Aldis lamp (to flash Morse code), exchanging ship name and passage details with ships that passed in the night.

After Suez

The Suez Canal had now re-opened after the failure of the British-led invasion the previous year. As the prime minister was swept from the political map, we made a left turn at Gibraltar into a glassy smooth Mediterranean, full-steam to Port Said (Egypt). Wars come and go, but given the chance, commerce treats obstacles like eels treat a weir.

Still, it was a mess. Although the canal had been cleared of wreckage following the conflict, there were plenty of signs of war damage. Port Said harbour area was littered with the remains of sunken vessels.

The Johnnie Walker sign in Port Said

Canny gilly-gilly

If Britannia had taken a beating, her legacy curiously endured. Johnnie Walker was still going strong in his swanky red coat and cane, dominating the local skyline as we moored in front of a huge advert for the iconic whisky. Soon, the bum-boats (local pedlar craft) swarmed alongside us like piglets round a sow, eager to sell their wares. Canny traders had all adopted British names. One called himself George Robey, an early Music Hall performer, while another introduced himself as "Sandy Mackenzie fae Aberdeen". Then the Gilly-Gilly men came aboard to perform their magic, making day-old chicks disappear before your eyes. You could take a wager with them but you'd never win. They'd have your ten shillings before blinking. I bought a couple of khaki shirts and pairs of shorts as I thought my whites were a bit conspicuous on this ship. Step by step, I was discarding all vestiges of *Orion* etiquette, as if Johnnie Walker had tossed away his top hat.

For years, Britain had operated the canal, justifying the war as protecting free passage after Egypt's abrupt nationalisation. But now, it was *our* ship that almost blocked it. Under the new masters, we had a Soviet pilot – our Cold War 'enemy' (though affable and friendly in person). All looked well until the heaving line on our stern rope parted and the wind swung us round to face in the wrong direction as we waited for a northward bound convoy to pass. It was a nail-biting moment. Urgently, I called the canal radio station to request immediate assistance – silence. Again, no response. Doubts invaded our minds. Were the authorities up to it: running such a vital trading artery on their own? The sight of an approaching tug finally provided our answer. Our fears swiftly evaporated in the desert as we proceeded on our way.

Aladdin's plagues

With the thermometer heading for boiling point as we left the canal, the Red Sea toasted our faces rouge. But there was a reward for our endurance – a stop in Aden (Yemen). This was an Aladdin's cave: Japanese tea sets, jewellery, Rolex watches, electric equipment, all at tax-free prices. I went ashore with the second mate to help him choose a nine waveband Pye Cambridge with good shortwave coverage. Top notch at the time; now fit for the *Antiques Roadshow*.

As we walked the streets, who should we meet but a young steward from *Orion*, also in the harbour. Quick as a conjurer, I pulled the old pipe I'd picked up in Glasgow from my pocket (see Chapter 3). "Give this to your junior third; he left it on the bus." No doubt, my grizzled old shipmate embellished the tale over the years in many a smoky room: "…and when I lost my pipe on the Clyde, y'll never believe it, the damn thing washed up in Aden a month later." A real Red Sea miracle.

Aden was also the scene of biblical plagues. A thick fog of fluttering locusts encrusted the ship as we departed, squeezing in wherever they found an open door or porthole. After a couple of days they abruptly left, as if on God's orders, only to be replaced with an even larger swarm of giant emperor dragonflies. In a gruesome turn, they started cannibalising each other, reputedly as the male only gets one chance of a bit of fun in his life-cycle and when he's finished the female kills him! Or perhaps he just expires from the effort.

Frying tonight

In this heat, you could understand the desire to drop dead. But the Red Sea was but a mere warm-up for the Persian Gulf where every part of the ship became hot to touch. The only cooling system we had was a paltry electric fan. The molten core of the furnace was my cabin. To get a decent sleep, I rigged a hammock on the monkey island (the roof of the wheelhouse). For six weeks, the noon temperature was never below 120°F (49°C) and once touched 126°F (52°C). You could fry an egg on the iron deck; even wood felt like burning coals to walk bare-foot on. By six a.m., we dropped to an almost 'chill' 90°F (39°C). Bliss it was when the wind blew from the north, blasting us with a hot, but mercifully dry, desert breeze. Otherwise, we swam in incessant sweat, endless day and sleepless night.

Weary, we reached the estuary. The S.S. *King Faisal II* lay at anchor where we stopped to pick up the Iraqi pilot. My Uncle Charlie had been pilot master based at Al Fao, but was now one of eight berthing masters at Harmaq, a small community directly opposite the port of Abadan. Charlie, Elsie and their youngest, four-year-old Maurice, came on board as we passed. I took them to the bridge to meet the Old Man and some of my shipmates. Maurice was more interested in the chief steward, who had some goodies in the fridge that even the crew didn't know about.

Twenty Thousand Leagues

The Shatt al-Arab from Al Fao to Basra

The house-boy

The winds of post-imperial change were whipping up a pretty stiff breeze by now, but the British expat could still enjoy many goodies. With an open invitation and the prospect of a long queue for a berth at Khorramshahr up river, I was soon picked up in a launch for a shore visit. The whole crew lined the rail to cheer me off, dripping with envy. The cool burr of air-conditioning would be the very breath of heaven.

No doubt, the colonels of the British Raj would have recognised the set up. Harmaq was a small hamlet spread out over a 12-acre site, right on the river bank. The harbour staff lived in substantial,

Barques, Sparks & Sharks

flat-roofed, brick houses, with a gardener who kept it all tidy and grew vegetables for them. Best of all, each had a large rooftop air conditioning unit that kept the interior down to 83°F, even if it was 40 degrees higher outside. Every family also had a 'house-boy' to do the housework and cooking. Charlie and Elsie had Hashim, a friendly 30-something who lived with his family in pretty basic conditions in a mud house a short distance up the river. No air con for him.

Every morning we nipped across the river to the Abadan Seaman's Club (technically on the Iranian side but it was, unofficially, an open border). It had good facilities for eating and drinking, a swimming pool and open-air film shows at night. The boys enjoyed a splash in the pool. The Indian Hindu doorman welcomed everybody with a welcoming, "*Ach-ha.*" Cash was not accepted. We purchased paper 'rial' tokens from the office. I started to learn a little Arabic, for you needed to be able to tell the boatman the number of the jetty you wanted, and how to buy a packet of smokes: "*Ashrin sikhara, min fethlek.*"

The locals treated us respectfully, if only because they were too well aware of the financial benefits that British business still brought to them. One day I was approached by a distinguished-looking Arab in his full robes. He obviously knew who I was and proudly introduced himself as head of the radio station. "Would you like to come round to see it?" Located in a small tower building on the river bank, it was smart and well equipped but not large, for although it handled all arrivals and departures from Abadan, this did not generate large amounts of radio traffic. Tea was served, Arab fashion, in small glasses, no milk and no sugar. His welcome was sweetness itself.

Meanwhile, a nomadic Iranian band was in town for a wedding. We were invited to hear them. Hand-woven Persian mats covered the earthen floor as we sat cross-legged in one of the mud houses, drinking tea while listening to half a dozen, male and female, entertainers. The instruments were fascinatingly appropriate to the region – constructed from one-gallon oil cans. A stiff wooden rod was attached vertically along one of the corners and a single tight string was attached to the top of the can near the opposite corner. It was played with a short bow consisting of a string stretched between the ends of a strong bent twig. At their invitation I had a go, but duly murdered one of my Orkney reels. The locals surely thought we had ears of concrete.

Aaaaah-lay

Pampering over – goodies all gone – it was soon back to back-bending work, unloading our cargo in Khorramshahr. It took three gruelling weeks, working overnight, starting around midnight and finishing by 10 a.m. in a race to beat the heat. We discharged into railway wagons, but as there was no shunting engine, the wagons were moved by hand. A gang of dockers positioned themselves round the truck and their head man called out a chant to co-ordinate the effort: "*Aaaaah-**lay**, aaaaah-**lay***", just like hauling a boat in Orkney ("*Aaaaaw-**heup**, aaaaaw-**heup***"). A welcome ice-boat came alongside every morning to fill our vacuum flasks and every available container. But it was usually consumed by noon, long before the ship got its daily hose-down with river water to try to douse the sticky, stinking heat.

To help unload, our iron bulwarks folded inwards to lie flat on the deck. One night, our colourful ex-convict, Able Seaman Flanagan, came back on board rather the worse for wear. It was the dockers' night off, so he stretched himself out on the hatch-cover and fell into a woozy sleep. Next morning, his body was found dead to the world after a 20-foot drop. His battered, black and bloodied limbs lay spread-eagled on the concrete pier after his sleepwalking, self-inflicted GBH. Miraculously, our man of iron was back at work, large as life, only a few days later.

We were tough. By the time we'd unloaded, our six-week stint in the Gulf made us scoff at the Hansa Line wimps berthed alongside, swooning with heat-stroke, even *with* air-con. Life in the furnace had forged our crew hard as horseshoes.

AC/DC

We worked hard, we played hard. Our second mate, Ernie, was a talented lad with an electric sense of humour who now set about putting a model ship in a standard light bulb (rather than a bottle). Using thin card, he fashioned a miniature ocean liner and pierced the portholes with a sharp needle. Placing a torch bulb inside the hull, it lit up the holes when connected to a battery. And Ernie said, *'Let there be light!'* But that wasn't enough. He got me to disconnect the ship's 110 volt DC supply from his cabin's lamp-holder and secretly connect it to a torch battery. The chief engineer was duly called in to admire his workmanship, when Ernie cheerfully exclaimed, "I wonder if it'll work if I plug into that lamp-holder?" Ducking for cover, the chief braced for fire and brimstone. But miracle of miracles, the damn thing worked!

Nature's miracle, the south-west monsoon ensured natural air-con down the Indian Ocean to Mauritius. In Port Louis, the mail arrived with a small tubular package for me. It was addressed to Marconi's office in Chelmsford and readdressed a couple of times to reach our Mauritian agent. Inside I found a certificate from the Ministry of Transport and Civil Aviation, written in ornate Gothic and copperplate, awarding me a diploma for special proficiency in Morse code communication. A slightly fishy footnote threatened legal consequences for failure to display it on my office wall. Ernie kept a poker-straight face (but no prosecution ensued for my flagrant non-compliance).

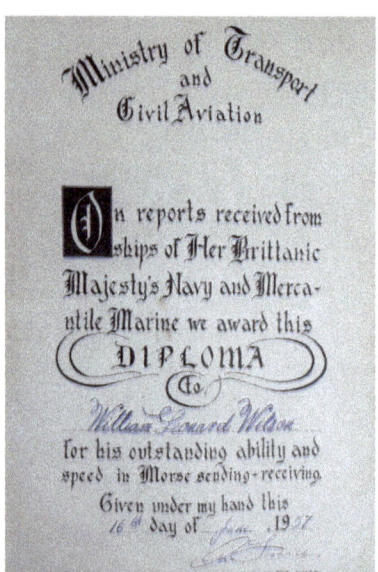

Pest control

We spent a week loading a full cargo of sugar but got more than we bargained for. The mate and the bosun spent a further week as Chief and Deputy Pest Controllers on a wild rat chase as we headed back to Suez. More sadly, someone had acquired a puppy in Port Louis and when the Old Man got wind of it, the poor dog went the same way as the rodents – 'over the wall'. At sea, the harsh and the hilarious are often twinned.

A ship on the ocean wave is a floating society with its own hierarchy and conflict resolution skills. The mate decided it was time the bridge companionways had a scrape and varnish and as a 'hands-on' man, he got hold of some tools to work together with our 'hard man' Flanagan, just outside my cabin door. They scraped and scraped, and then scraped a bit more, till words were spoken – sharp words. A commotion flared. Flanagan let rip: "Say that again and ah'll f'n kill ye!" I peeped out to see a fist of a face, eyes ablaze, poised with the heavy tool quivering like a dagger above his head. But the mate didn't flinch. He kept calm and carried on, as cool as Nelson at Trafalgar, before slipping quietly away, dignity and body intact. Doubtless, Flanagan would get a DR (decline to report) in his discharge book to add to his GBH.

Discharge

Moods, of course, switch like the wind. As we passed through the Med, sailing up the coast of Portugal, there was the usual outbreak of 'The Channels': the condition prevailing among a ship's crew as they start to get near home. Everybody goes about their work with a good-humored smile and a song. And unlike poor Flanagan, my discharge book would be in pretty good shape. I'd left home in January fresh from college. By October, I had served on ships great and small with 80,000 miles (20,000+ nautical leagues) under my belt – the

Barques, Sparks & Sharks

R.M.S. *St Ola*
(Ian Heddle, Orkney Image Library)

equivalent of twice round the equator, crossing the line six times. Homeward bound, I felt I was a man of the world. Britannia's post-Suez confidence had taken a hit but, professionally, I was on the up.

And so were my guts. Boarding the ferry for Orkney, my sea-leg confidence met the Pentland Firth. As I hung over the side of the *St Ola*, spewing my own personal discharge, I heard a voice behind me. It was 'Dusty' Clouston, the ferry's bosun: "Are ye sure yer been tae sea, or is that jeust a story yer tellin' us?"

5. The Wild West

My name rattled out in Morse: "We're sending you to join T&J Harrison's *Philosopher*." I didn't realise how privileged I was, for it was a company usually reserved for more senior men. Our first port of call would be La Guaira. I had to ask, "Where's that?" They pointed west – "Venezuela."

S.S. *Philosopher*. Radio callsign MAQV
Built on the Clyde as *Empire Addison* in 1942. 7,002 g.r.t.
(The Allen Collection)

Empire class

Privileged it may have been, but S.S. *Philosopher* was an Empire class wartime vessel, utterly spartan. My cabin had just space for a chair between the bunk and chest of drawers. The officers were mainly from

Liverpool and round about – second mate from Northumberland and third engineer, Tegwyn Jones, from Wales, while the chief steward, Bobby Breen, was a Scouser through and through. Socially, we were also 'Empire class': the catering staff, engine-room greasers and the 'crowd' were all West Indian, engaged to transport a complex general cargo to a variety of ports, all managed by our purser, Mr. Prosser, from North London. He will drop in on us again, in due course.

The company was variously known as 'Hungry Harrison's' or 'Two of Fat and One of Lean' (after the cheapest cuts of meat), due to their distinct white-red-white bands on a black funnel. I am pleased to say they didn't live up to their reputation as the food was rather above average. So, we were privileged after all, but the *Philosopher* was no speedboat. We cruised across the Atlantic at a puttering 8 knots: painfully slow but standard cargo-speed for the 1950s.

Privileges for some

La Guaira welcomed us with an impressive display by pelicans as they gorged themselves on fish from the harbour. They'd dive in – beak first – always facing in the opposite direction as they surfaced. Venezuela was often that kind of place. Grab what you can and watch your back.

Ports of call in the Caribbean

The Wild West

Venezuela's capital, Caracas, was about 20 miles up in the mountains, so I hopped on the bus to explore. The shanty-town poverty was barely believable as we approached the city, stacked up in front of me like a cliff of egg-boxes. By contrast, the city centre was very modern and expensive looking. Privileges for some.

The shanty-town approach to Caracas

The city centre, Caracas

Little Holland

After a short hop to Puerto Cabello, we headed to Willemstad in Curacao, part of the Netherlands Antilles, just like a fruit-pastel slice of 'Little Holland'. It offered an extensive, totally enclosed harbour with large oil storage and refining facilities. The entrance channel, 500 feet wide by 1 mile long, ran through the town centre, connected by a miraculously antique pontoon bridge that opened to allow ships into the harbour where we now docked, snugly inside.

The pontoon bridge in Willemstad
(Willem van de Poll via Wikimedia Commons)

The Dutch had a characteristically well-organised approach to trade of all types. 'Campo Alegre', a few miles from Willemstad, consisted of a set of smart-looking wooden houses behind a high barbed wire security fence, originally the site of a World War II US army barracks. A sign at the entrance instructed patrons to leave their knives and hand guns at the desk – which they presumably did politely and without fuss – all in order to enjoy the lively music that rang out from bars, thus enhancing the experience of a good night out, without necessarily partaking of the main course. (I was well warned about 'houses of ill-repute' and red light districts before I left home.) No drinking and driving either: taxis did a brisk trade, ceasing only when the COVID19 outbreak forced its closure in 2020.

Pirates and viggies

If life was 'fat' in Curacao, it could be very lean in Venezuela – at least, some parts of it. After a week in the orderly Dutch speaking town, we headed for rural Punta Cardon on a peninsula joined to the mainland by a narrow isthmus at the outer entrance to Lake Maracaibo. Apart from an oil storage depot, the land was barren, just rock and sand with hardly a scrap of vegetation. A short walk inland revealed a sparse population living in broken-down shacks with a few goats and hens running around – an extreme, hand-to-mouth existence, cheek-by-jowl with a gushing source of wealth.

We were in *'Pirates of the Caribbean'* territory. Henry Morgan, the notorious Welsh privateer of the 17th century, famously deceived the Spanish garrison of Maracaibo into training their guns in the wrong direction before he sneaked in below them to raid the town.

The city was now a Hispanic Wild West! Bars thronged to live music and dancing into the night. Our South African apprentice made a name for himself when the floor suddenly cleared to reveal him and his partner putting on a racy performance in the middle of the floor. Whooped into a frenzy, they eventually turned, red-faced and panting, to acknowledge the echoing applause. "She started it!" he protested. But by the early hours, it was the cops that tended to finish it. Anyone unsteady on their feet got dotted on the head with a baton and thrown into the back of their wagon. It was time to go.

Today's 'pirates and privateers' were the drillers of Lake Maracaibo, a huge shallow expanse, measuring close to 100 miles long by 70 miles wide that was – and still is – a major source of Venezuela's oil wealth. Heading for Lagunillas on the east side of the lake, we navigated between spindly rows of oil wells extending to a hazy infinity.

Navigating between the oil wells in Lake Maracaibo

You know it's the 'Wild West' if you need an armed posse when unloading your cargo. Everything had to be under lock and key now, with an escort of half a dozen vigilantes, dressed in battle kit, rifles and hand guns, to ensure law and order. *Viggies*, we called them. Our hired dockers camped under tarpaulins slung from the derrick hooks on the forward hatches and the *viggies* lived down aft.

Posh Mr. Prosser

Thoroughly out of place among the roughnecks and desperadoes, our very proper purser (posh Mr. Prosser) was an ex P&O man with a demeanour and accent that set him apart. On Christmas Eve, the hatches were closed and the derrick hook was hanging from the deck above, while the rest of us sat having a few beers, spinning yarns as only seafarers can, under the chief steward's customary regime of alcoholic generosity. Out of the boozy haze, an apparition appeared like Santa coming down the chimney: posh Mr. Prosser had become 'one of the lads', swinging down on the derrick hook, startlingly starkers! We cheered with a chorus of, "What shall we do with the drunken sailor?" Next day, the actual 'lads' still had to work so that the officers could sit down to turkey, Christmas pud and all the trimmings. Our West Indian cook and stewards really pulled out the stops. As a reward, we seated them in our saloon on Boxing Day and *we* served them *their* Christmas dinner. 'Doc' (the chef) still had to do the cooking though. Ships rarely shake off their ancient hierarchies.

A stern-wheeled paddle steamer pushing barges in Lake Maracaibo

Down to Bachaquero, we sailed into a sepia-tinged age, drifting across the lake through scenes from a Turner painting. As we puttered along, antique stern-wheel paddle steamers were still in daily operation, pushing monstrous barges before them like heaving elephants.

A stern-wheeler with barge alongside near Bachaquero

Barques, Sparks & Sharks

Coups, conquistadors and commies

Our dockers and viggies were due to be dropped off in Maracaibo as we headed for Cartagena (Colombia) when the news flash reached us. Venezuelan strongman, Marcos Pérez Jiménez, had fled and the army was patrolling the streets – we had just dodged a coup!

The military had long ruled these lands – or tried to – since the conquistadors. Cartagena was originally established by the Spaniards in 1533 in the early days of colonisation and piracy. As we gazed up, the immense and forbidding city fortification (Castle San Felipe de Barajas) held the key to the riches of South America – exporting silver and importing slaves. The fort was an architectural *viggie*, hewn from the bare rock. The second mate and I set off, tagging along behind a party of nuns who were, somewhat incongruously, receiving a guided tour through a network of tunnels in the fortified walls. Brute force and piety were an everyday mix in such a precarious region.

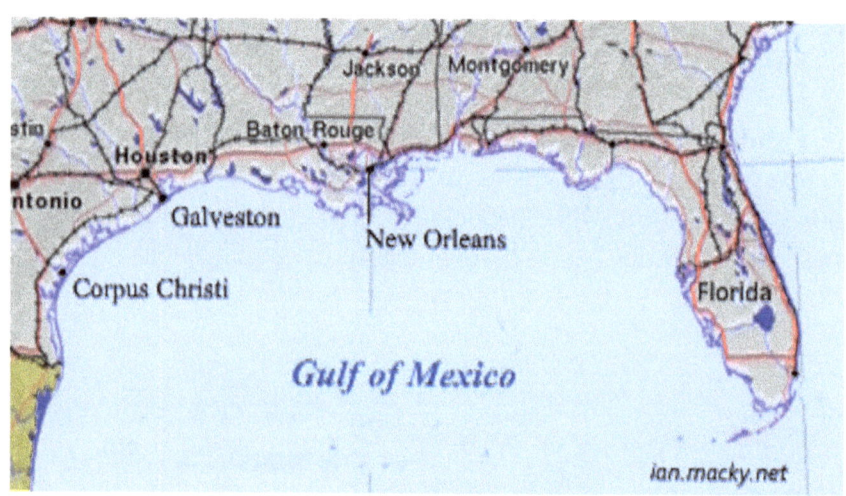

The Gulf of Mexico

A significantly cooler atmosphere was expected as we proceeded up the Gulf coast to load for home, calling first at Corpus Christi

(Texas), about a hundred miles from the Mexican border. 'Uncle Sam' stood lantern-jawed as the whole crew were interviewed by US Immigration. In a sure sign of the times, the classic Cold War question was posed to all: "Are you, or have you been, a member of the Communist Party?" A quick denial and you were in.

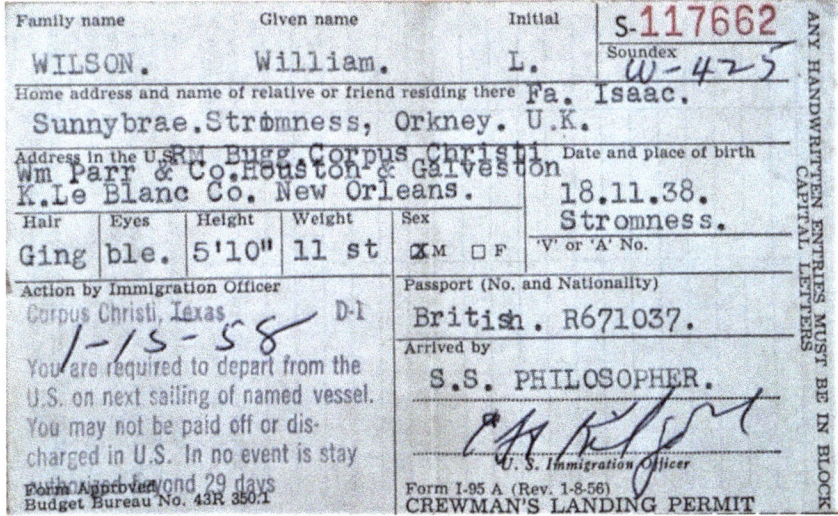

The US Immigration landing permit

'Wetbacks'

The immigration officer was accompanied by a member of the Border Patrol, in full uniform with a six-gun and bandolier of bullets – literally dressed to kill. His main task was patrolling the Mexican border, catching the 'wetbacks' who regularly swam the Rio Grande to enter the US. He proudly demonstrated the workings of his revolver and the different types of ammunition. "This bullet here will stop a man at 50 feet." He might have fainted on the spot if I'd mentioned Britain's unarmed constabulary.

Of course, we wouldn't be needing any *viggies* to protect us here. During a quiet drink in a bar one night with pals, I returned from out back when I found myself in a tight scrum of half a dozen young Texans. They were chatty – even a shade over-insistent – inviting me to come to a 'party' with them. I humoured them as an involuntary spasm of tension darted like forked lightning between us. Would this be the kind of party that left me penniless – possibly lifeless – dumped in the ditch? I stalled, hoping mightily that somebody would come along NOW. The scrum leader persisted, "Say, guy, where are *you* from?" With no escape possible, I blurted it out: "Scotland!" He swivelled sharply to his mates. "Hey, this guy's OK," – and they all melted miraculously away. Perhaps they heard that Scots are made from girders. Or was it my look of Viking menace?

'The Big Easy'

The Mississippi paddle steamer *President* at New Orleans
(Murphy Library Special Collections/ARC, University of Wisconsin-La Crosse)

Like the old plantation days, we loaded bales of cotton before moving up the coast, first to Galveston and then our last port of call, the jazzy, sassy city of New Orleans. A hundred miles up the Mississippi, it was just before Mardi Gras when 'the Big Easy' is still an easy place to like. After a wander round the French Quarter and along Canal Street we settled on Bourbon Street with all its bars and fantastic jazz bands reminiscent of Louis Armstrong, Duke Ellington and Count Basie. We soaked it all in for the price of a beer.

Blind triangulation

It was time to head home, straight into the realm of pseudo-scientific superstition: the 'Bermuda Triangle'. Already in the Florida Strait, we hit a fierce south-easterly, with a huge sea coming up on our starboard quarter. Even from the bridge, the horizon was dipping out of sight as we wallowed in the trough till – all fury spent – a smothering fog rolled in. Creeping along at 3 knots, our siren blasted the crew sleepless every two minutes. Without any radar, we were feeling our way blindly when a large 'hot-rod' Panamanian freighter charged across our bows – barely a tanker-length ahead – its radar turning merrily with siren mute. But what can you do? Eventually, we reverted to long range radio, counting out dots and dashes before cross-referencing with a table of 'consol' bearings that would guide us home, like a bat in the dark.

Almost lost, virtually blind, our voyage had still been a real eye-opener – from nuns to vigilantes, jazz bars to shanty towns. We dodged battle scars and near misses, fuelled along the way by oil and booze. Too much perhaps. The chief steward's on-board drinking culture had spun yarns into the night that sometimes took the privilege of serving on S.S. *Philosopher* a little too far.

My cod

Yet, the oddest thing of all: we had just passed through the Bermuda Triangle from the land of pirates, Blackbeard and Henry Morgan, but the spookiest, fishiest tale I ever heard was told, not by an ancient mariner, but by my carriage companion – Mr. John Abrach Mackay – on the train slowly winding us up through the Northern Highlands:

Barques, Sparks & Sharks

Back in the day, constructing the road from Thurso to John O'Groats, the workmen came across ancient graves containing skeletons. I was a Caithness County Councillor at the time and went out to inspect the scene. Spotting a human tooth lying in the ground, I picked it up and stuck it in my pocket as a souvenir. A few days later, I had to go over to Orkney on business. I booked the hotel in advance and when I arrived, I found the landlady in a state of distress as her husband had died suddenly that day. I offered to move, but she insisted she would honour all her bookings. That night, I drifted off into a sound sleep, only to be roused at 4 a.m. by a great commotion. The hotel was on fire. I grabbed a coat and got out into the street where we all stood shivering till the fire brigade extinguished the flames. When we were allowed back in, there was no more sleep.

As the day dawned, I set off back to the ferry. It was a perfect morning but when we passed Hoy Sound, the wind suddenly got up and was a full gale in no time. Captain Swanson had never experienced such a storm-tossed passage. In the middle of the Firth, the ship creaked ominously.

Would we all drown? I suddenly remembered the tooth in my pocket. I took it out, tossed it into the sea and, would you believe it, the wind calmed to a whisper and the waters turned flat. The voyage ended in perfect conditions ... but that's not the end of the story. Next day, I was walking by the harbour, when I met a fisherman who says to me, "John, ye see what I took oot o' the belly o' a cod this morning?" And there, right in the palm of his hand was ... the tooth!

The crew of the *Philosopher*, the nuns, the viggies, the jazzmen and perhaps even posh Mr. Prosser would like to confirm that this was the tooth, the whole tooth and nothing but the tooth, so help me cod – and if you think we're done with wild, *fang-tastic* stories, wait till you get to Chapter 6.

6. Shell Shocks

Their crewman poked his head above the hatch, sprinted to the fo'c's'le, grabbed a heavy hammer and released his anchor chain – too late! Our oil tanker, *Hindsia*, heavily laden, struck their starboard bow with a metallic scrunch. I was on deck, watching unconcerned when we started to drift sideways towards a large Everard's coaster lying at anchor. Surely our tug would take up the slack; surely, a ship of our size and weight would never … but, in the end, we hardly even felt the impact. Instead, our victim heeled over, teetering at a perilous angle. Would it …? My chest heaved. The crew must have thought their end had come as they emerged like beetles from a burning log, white faced and shaken. Phew!

Raking it in

Tankers were trouble: the lengthy spells at sea, the rapid turnarounds, usually in inhospitable ports, with the ever present danger – a spark, a spill – while constantly having to scan ahead for civil strife, market shock, the tumble of the dollar or just counting the endless waves. But it paid – 25% extra – and if they were going to shell out, I was going to rake it in.

At only two years old S.T.S. *Hindsia* was no rust bucket, driven at a decent 16 knots by steam turbine engines producing 7500 s.h.p. The spacious accommodation on board was a welcome bit of luxury after my previous compact quarters. We even carried a library of cine films – *Casablanca, From Here to Eternity, The African Queen*, etc. – manned by Sparks, your chief projectionist. In warmer climes, I'd set up on the lee side of the boat deck for a weekly show, with an exchange of films at Shell depots round the world. Who needs popcorn!

S.T.S. *Hindsia*. Radio callsign GTMQ
Built in 1955 by Vickers Armstrong, Barrow-in Furness. 12,212 g.r.t.

The *hindsia magnifica* that gave the ship its name

See-saw and slings

Directed to "Key West for orders", we hiked across a mountain range of Atlantic peaks. Our dining saloon was aft, but the sea was heaving it like a see-saw, 30 feet at a time: *Seeeeee-saaaaww*. You had to plan your movements strategically. The ship had a flying bridge that connected the centre-castle to the after accommodation, but getting there risked a soaking, or worse, as heavy seas smashed continuously across the main deck 10 feet below. We'd watch for a lull and then dash as far as the mast (for a small shelter) only to wait for another lull before the final sprint. It should have been an Olympic event.

Initially, we dodged around the Caribbean and the Gulf of Mexico – Bullen Bay, Willemstad, Aruba, Punta Cardon, Port Arthur, Port Elizabeth, Houston – before heading our way out to the Philippines through the Panama Canal. This is where we earned our higher pay, enduring long spells afloat while praying that we might have a mid Pacific stop as it was a 10,000 mile journey. And sure enough, we hit the jackpot: "Proceed Honolulu for bunkers [i.e. fuel] and water." We docked with our nose sticking almost into the main street but could only poke it in for half a day – barely time to hula-hoop or even nab a pineapple.

After two blank weeks of blue-grey ocean, we finally reached the riotous confusion of Manilla, rejoicing in its rumbustious streets choked with ancient rickshaws and the wildest, technicolor Jeeps as they honked their way through the mayhem. But it wasn't long before we set off for Pulau Bukom, a small island about three miles off Singapore, as placid as a swan. The whole place was taken up by a Shell refinery and its associated oil storage tanks. It was a short ferry and taxi run from there to the centre of Singapore where the large Chinese quarter simply buzzed with commercial activity, day and night. At the still centre of the city stood the resplendent Raffles Hotel, the colonial bastion where we went for our gin sling, back in the days when – unlike now – it was still actually by the sea. In Singapore, you blink and it's changed.

Bullets, bottles and chip-pans

Captain Hunt left us in Singapore to be replaced by an affable Geordie, Captain Jamieson. No one wants a leader with an itchy finger on the trigger, so when I got the job of typing up a revised inventory for the handover, I was intrigued by the entry "one handgun and six rounds of ammunition", marked down from seven rounds at the previous transfer. Who was in his cross-hairs, I wondered? I got on well enough with him, but he was aloof and full of self-importance. He liked to make his presence felt and to give orders, though I witnessed one of the Tyne dockers putting him firmly in his place with a stern "You're not on your ship now, Captain!" By contrast, Captain Jamieson was a very fine man but, like many a seafarer, rather fond of the bottle – though he had a temper too, as we shall see.

From Singapore we headed like a heat-seeking missile up the Sumatra Strait, across the Bay of Bengal and through the Arabian Gulf to the infamous Persian Gulf and Abadan. I knew it would be hot as a chip pan – I had already rigged up my bed on deck – but at least Uncle Charlie would be there with a royal welcome.

On long voyages, a passing ship is a friend, especially if an actual friend, or even a relative, is aboard, no matter how distant. Any time that I came across a Bank Line boat on the radio I'd ask for the skipper's name, hoping that my granny's brother's wife's brother, Archie Williamson, might be aboard. But he never was.

As the next Bank vessel steamed down the Shatt al-Arab, we dutifully came out on deck to wave with faint expectations ... completely unaware that Captain Archie had just passed by, steaming towards the horizon.

Shell Shocks

The Persian Gulf

Kingdom come

But we might have waved for the very last time. At Sitra (Bahrain), we passed the shattered torso of M.V. *Seistan*, gruesomely sunk earlier that year. Heading for Khorramshahr, a fire broke out in the hold, so they put in to Sitra to extinguish it. While they were discharging cargo to try to reach the source of the fire, a massive explosion took place, breaking the ship in two and killing most on board, as well as some of the shore personnel, plus the crew of a tug that was alongside. In all, 57 lost their lives, with just 18 survivors, including the mate and his wife and young daughter. Amazingly, the culprit was two crates of toe puff (used to manufacture shoes) that had been wrongly stowed in the hold, along with a quantity of high explosives. Innocent and playful sounding, it was the kindling that blasted them all to kingdom come.

M.V. *Seistan* before the explosion
(Rodney Towers)

… and the aftermath
(Rodney Towers)

It was now we received the news that Iraq itself had blown up. The BBC announced that King Faisal II and his family had been massacred in a military coup. This was personal as well as political. Six years previously, Uncle Charlie had been pilot master for the Shatt al-Arab, often using the S.S. *King Faisal II* which lay at anchor off the estuary and doubled as the Iraqi Royal Yacht. He took the young monarch, then aged 17, on a Gulf tour to visit his ruling royal neighbours, during which the king presented him with an inscribed gold watch at the end of the voyage. But with British influence ebbing, a swirl of undercurrents was sucking Iraq into choppier water, now without its pilot.

Cloak 'n' dagger

Like many a soldier, seafarers seek adventure, only to crave safety shortly thereafter. Returning peacefully to the relative security of Singapore, we headed for the tropical bliss of Tandjung Uban, a small idyllic island just south of the city, utterly blind to any danger and menace. But Shell HQ was on edge. *Hindsia*'s sister ship *San Flaviano* (run by a Shell subsidiary) had just been bombed from the air in Balikpapan harbour (Indonesia) to scare off foreign trade – all part of an ongoing insurgency against President Sukarno that culminated in the mid-1960s.

S.T.S. *San Flaviano*, a sister ship to S.T.S. *Hindsia*
(Kees Helder. Helderline.com)

… and after the bombing
(Kees Helder. Helderline.com)

Astonishingly, it later emerged the attack was actually carried out by the CIA, with tacit British support. For our own safety, we were now required to report our noon position daily to Head Office in London. Although we were on a higher pay rate, it seems we had to be protected from the skulduggery of our own government.

It was all getting a bit cloak 'n' dagger. Shell sent all their communication in company code, so Captain Jamieson handed me his first position report together with the cypher book. "You just code it and send it every day after this." I did so, but a sixth sense made me check, only to find that he had replaced the code for latitude 'south' with 'north'. Officially, we were half way up a mountain! Given the growing tension, London management would be shaken, even stirred into action, had I not quickly sent a corrected version. Our current course, somewhere between low comedy and high drama, meant stranger things had happened and would do so again. But surely our captain wasn't on the CIA payroll ... or had he drunk one bottle too many?

Back in the Pacific, we ended up in what Captain Cook likened to Scotland during a ray of sunshine, but was now the French territory of New Caledonia, where we moored ourselves in a deserted bay near the capital, Nouméa.

S.T.S. *Hindsia* discharging into a sub-sea pipeline in New Caledonia

Shell Shocks

The view from the hill above our anchorage, with Nouméa in the background

Stony ground

After long days at sea, Nouméa was as tempting as Venice, Las Vegas and Monte Carlo blurred into one. In the morning, we persuaded the second mate to take us up to the capital with the ship's own boat. He nodded. After all, we were young, but responsible. What could go wrong? By evening, we dutifully returned to the pick up point, only to find that Captain Jamieson had decided he would like a shore trip too. Unfortunately, as he landed, the Harbour Authority decided to take an interest, strip-searching the lifeboat for illicit goods, drugs, whatever, even examining the boat's emergency rations. Rarely disgruntled, poor old Captain Jamieson, after all the stress of the day, was very far from gruntled. And although it's seldom wise to annoy a bureaucrat, especially on their home turf, it's positively risqué if you're a visiting Englishman *en France*.

Our two Geordies, captain and second mate, were promptly marched off to the Harbour Office for interrogation where, not surprisingly, it would be hard to find an official who wouldn't take action if you rammed your foot through his door panel. The Old Man duly spent the night in a francophone slammer till the shipping agent bailed him out the next day. We departed Nouméa in silence. A few days later, I delivered the news of his fine – in stonier silence.

Gums

Leaving our blushes in New Caledonia, a peaceful stretch of nothingness was something of a relief. But at sea, you always have to be on the lookout as you never know what might bite you in the behind – or in the ship's log. This is not, in fact, a bible-sized volume filled in with quill pen. It's a heavy brass device about 20 inches long in the form of a streamlined impeller that is towed behind the ship on a long line. The log spins as it moves through the water, turning a dial on-board to record the miles travelled. But our second mate noticed that the iron bracket that supports the ship-board end of the log-line had been severely bent. Clearly, we had snagged something heavy. Very heavy. But what could it be? Hauling the log in, he found the evidence. Embedded in the line, about a foot above the log, was a startlingly sinister needle-sharp tooth. You've heard of *Jaws*, but look out for 'Gums'.

Ship's log impeller

Iron Queen

By now, I was no stranger to the South Pacific – how many blue-eyed northerners had visited Fiji three times in less than two years – all before the age of 20? This time we were moored in a totally deserted bay at Vuda Point in order to discharge into a sub-sea pipeline just off the coral fringed shore, backed by an explosion of coconut palms. We were having a few welcome beers, soaking up the blissful tranquillity, when a young Fijian emerged from the undergrowth wielding a machete. As quick as a cat, he hacked off a dozen coconuts from the tree-top before inviting us to visit his village nearby.

We came upon a small settlement. The houses were mainly traditional grass buildings with a thick grassy thatch. Some were built of timber weatherboard. The most impressive was a wooden house with roof shingles, home of the village King and Queen. Our guide explained that no one was allowed to have their head above the King, so it was the practice to duck down by bending your knees when approaching him. The accession of a taller monarch might have dispensed with the issue, but as he was away on business, we did not have to worry. Instead, we would be taken to visit his consort. The Queen invited us in as she was doing her ironing. Rather than inserting a red hot coal, her appliance was heated within by solid blocks of *metafuel* that burned with a near invisible flame when lit with a match, glowing radiant like squares of white chocolate.

The house décor was a mix of modern and traditional. The spacious lounge took up most of the dwelling, offering the ambiance of a small hall with a nice polished hardwood floor. It was obvious who was in charge of the interior decoration. The walls were festooned with a variety of ladies' leather handbags, each alternating with a large crescent cluster of impressive cowrie shells, symbolising status and wealth, both modern and traditional. Ironing done, the Queen made us tea, serving it in delicate china cups. After we gently took our leave, some of the villagers suggested, if we cared to come back that evening, they would organise a *kava* ceremony for us, which we duly agreed to.

Mbula

When we returned, a large group of all ages gathered with us in a wooden building that served as a community centre. A man had obtained a small cloth bag of *krok* (the ground root of a native tree) for making *kava*. He placed the bag in a *tanoa*, a large wooden ceremonial bowl full of water and kneaded it thoroughly for several minutes until all the good was extracted. And that was it. *Cheers!*

But it all had to be consumed in the right way – the Fijian way. We duly sat cross-legged in a circle on the floor, and after some informal welcoming speeches the ceremony began. A half coconut shell was filled from the bowl and passed to the first person on the server's left. The recipient clapped once, taking the cup in both hands while calling out *"mbula"* ('give life') before downing the cup in one go. Then the whole company clapped three times before the cup returned for a refill and on to the next in line, clockwise till the bowl was empty, all while accompanied by much chatter and entertainment. Candidly, *kava* is an acquired – or more likely, an unacquired – taste, like earthy (even muddy) water, consumed to enhance the mood rather than the palate. The numbing taste and rhythmic ritual had a mellowing effect – no boozy antics in Fiji. They could easily have hacked off our heads and we still would have smiled. And so would they.

Kava-dreams

Fijian aggression was instead channelled into rugby, which young men played wild and barefoot. In 1958 few people outside the islands knew of their prowess, so their declared ambition to compete internationally was easily dismissed as a pleasant but mind numbing *kava*-dream. A quick fast-forward shows the national team reaching the quarter finals of the rugby world cup in 1987 and again in 2007, defeating Wales in what the *Guardian* reported as a "glorious outpouring of sporting folly" by the ever flamboyant Flying Fijians!

Shocks and sometimes follies, great and small, were becoming the 'post-Suez' norm, even if we only half aware of it.

Heading thoughtfully home, we passed the Egyptians toiling away on improvement and widening of the canal (without the French and British), working not with machines but with hundreds of men, like slaves of the pharaohs, picking away with shovels and wheelbarrows.

Shell Shocks

Widening the Suez Canal with picks and shovels

Through sheer raw effort, they too wished to pursue their own '*kava-dream*', to be masters of their own fate. Along with the Fijians, the Indonesians (and even the Iraqis), each in their own different ways, were struggling to make their mark on the world which my own seafaring forebears – for better and for worse – had dominated for so long.

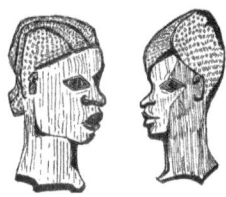

7. White Rabbits, Dark Fears

Deep Sea Plunderings deeply plundered my ten-year-old mind. The book still sits like a tombstone upon my shelf, but as a child, the very thought of it ignited the wildest, rampant imaginings. Captain Halcrow's 16 seafaring 'tales of fact' were dedicated "To the Memory of Good Companionship and Stirring Years Spent in the Oil Rivers of Southern Nigeria". His blood-spattering account of *Ju-Ju Vengeance* remains indelible. I jumped at my own shadow after reading it.

Fact or fiction, Halcrow certainly knew his stuff. He'd been master of the steamer *Iddo* in the Nigerian coastal service, manned by British officers with a mixture of locals, the dominant being the Kroo (or Kru) who, from Sierra Leone to Nigeria, were noted (like Orcadians) for their prowess on the sea. Halcrow's story was a spine-chilling tale of black magic and the human sacrifice of one of his ship's crew during a *ju-ju* ritual, deep in the jungle one eerie, moonlit African night. As I crept up the stairs to bed – heart thumping, sweat dripping – I'd surely have plunged into an epileptic fit if I'd known, only ten years later, I'd make two voyages into the same jungle rivers with the Kroo-boys, sons and grandsons of Halcrow's men.

In the spring of 1959, I had joined 'Paddy' Henderson & Co., of Glasgow at £45 per month, a significant pay rise, for which I would also be responsible for signing on the crew while looking after their wages and cash advances. Henderson (in conjunction with the Elder Dempster Line) dominated the West Africa trade on this coast, from the Gambia to the Congo.

M.V. *Kumba*. Radio callsign GVRR
Built by Lithgow's, on the Clyde in 1958. 5438 g.r.t.
(P Henderson archive)

The *Kumba* was a new ship of 5,438 tons gross, named after a town in Cameroon. Although not big, it was a well-equipped, modern vessel, with good accommodation and food. The officers were British (including two pursers seconded from Elder Dempster to keep tabs on the cargo manifest) and the 'crowd' were African, from Sierra Leone. Socially, little had changed since the days of *Deep Sea Plunderings*.

Dodgy crew

Like a certain young Alice, I found myself following white rabbits into my latest wonderland – 'darkest Africa'. Childishness aside, they were, in fact, for a modern medical research facility in Lagos, along with a mix of everything from manufactured goods to bagged meal.

White Rabbits, Dark Fears

The rabbits were carried in cages on the boat deck; whereas for the journey home, we would take on palm oil, copra, plywood and a huge deck cargo of iroko and sapele logs from every English speaking port and every navigable creek, bar one. We called at Bathurst (now Banjul) in The Gambia, then on to Freetown in Sierra Leone, where I was sent ashore to pay off and sign on a new crew. Mission accomplished, or so I thought. Captain Grassick knocked on my cabin door that night. "Sparks, it's not your fault. I should have warned you, but you've signed on six DRs." Not doctors, but men with 'decline to report' in the character column of their discharge books. I winced but we sailed on regardless, with our dodgy crew. We'd have to look out.

We hugged the coast, loaded like a giant turtle. After Freetown (Sierra Leone), it was off to Monrovia (Liberia), then on to Ghana (Takoradi, Cape Coast and Accra), followed by several stops in Nigeria (Lagos, Burutu, Warri, Sapele, Abonema, Port Harcourt, Calabar), then all the way to Victoria and Tiko, in Cameroon.

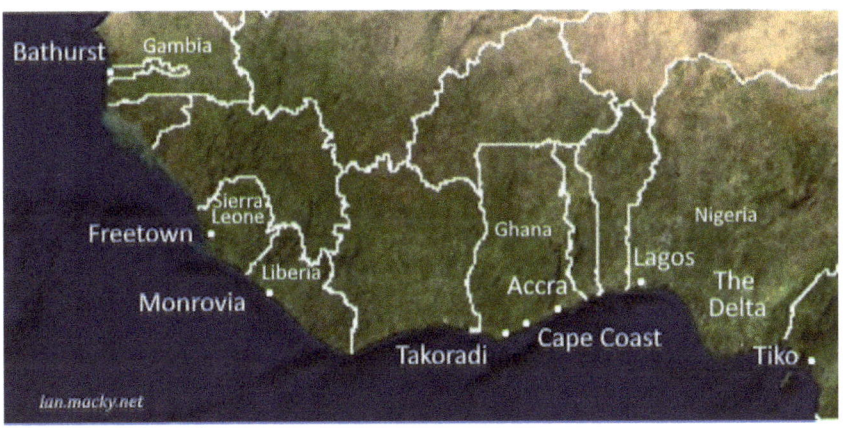

The West African coast from The Gambia to Cameroon

No monsters and magic from my childhood could stop our progress, the only enemy being the mosquito – nature's little vampire. Defences were ready, including daily doses of *paludrine* to protect us from the dreaded malaria and a fine mesh fitted on every porthole and doorway.

Meanwhile, a counter-attack was planned – cabins armed with an insecticide spray gun. To feed our 'troops', we caught silverfish (not unlike a small barracuda) in the harbour at Takoradi, though my first attempts to catch them failed when they bit right through the line, before a six-inch trace of fine wire sorted the problem.

No sissies

Unloading cargo was not unlike the D-Day landings. Incredibly, there were no actual harbours at Accra and Cape Coast (Ghana), so we had to lie at anchor a couple of miles offshore and discharge bags of meal into our surfboats (clinker-built, double-ended craft, built in Liverpool).

A surfboat approaches the ship.
Note the oil drum for buoyancy below the helmsman's feet

The original plan was to fit them with engines, but this proved impractical for landing through heavy surf onto a beach, so the African crews improvised as they knew best – a steersman standing on a platform aft and eight men with 'ducks-feet' paddles, chanting to keep time as they powered along. It was a job for 'special forces' – for warriors.

Loading was a particularly hazardous operation as the boats peaked and plunged at least 6 feet on the swell. The winch-man's timing needed to be impeccable. If he dropped the load as the boat was rising, it was sunk, with cargo adrift and nine men swimming. Life-jackets were for sissies.

Righting a surfboat after a sinking

Barques, Sparks & Sharks

The boat was recovered with the winch, while the crew gathered their paddles and bottom boards, climbed in and got on with the job as though nothing had happened.

Retrieving the surfboat

Dodgy Kroo

My long-anticipated encounter with the Kroo (Kru) also occurred as if nothing had happened. In the creeks to the east, we lacked manpower to handle the cargo, so we engaged a party of Kroo-boys in Lagos who would remain with us until our return to the Nigerian capital. Labour being cheap, we carried a large number of them, working under the command of their headman, while camped on top of the hatch-boards under tarpaulin 'tents' slung from the derrick hooks. One was engaged as *dhobyman*, relieving us of laundry duties so our whites were returned blindingly clean, immaculately pressed.

Despite the good work, we were on alert. Keys were regularly used from now on, as our 'dodgy crew' feared it was the Kroo that were dodgy. My mind slipped back to the tales of Captain Halcrow and the *ju-ju* magic – wasn't his man spirited away through a locked door?

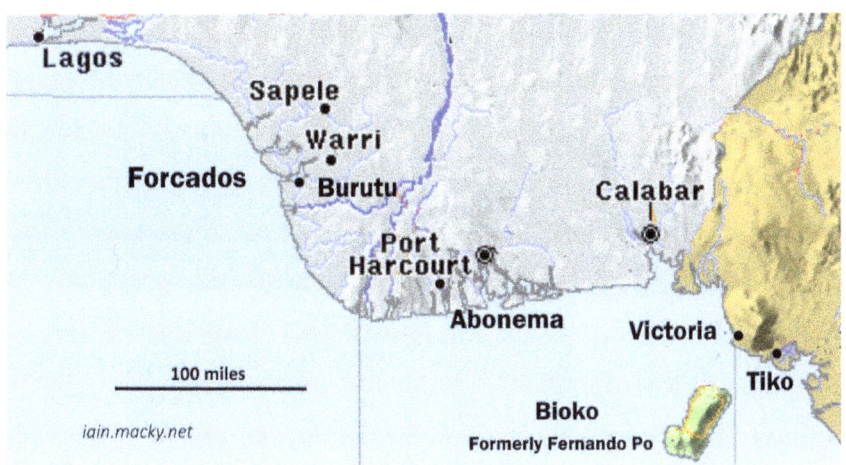

The Niger Delta

The labyrinth

Entering the western side of the Niger Delta at Forcados, we anchored in the river to await the pilot. The still heat rendered the water like glass, while all around a shimmering steam rose from the jungle, deathly quiet save for the odd excited scream of monkeys and exotic birds. Human life was utterly banished from the scene, or so we thought, until a dugout containing a woman and child approached from nowhere. "Dash me, Johnnie," she shouted repeatedly, till we threw down some empty cans, bars of soap and other items that might be useful. The child thrashed about in search of anything that didn't float while, high on another plane, we viewed the scene as a puppet performance, rather than an opportunity for benevolence.

The bush pilot arrived shortly, also in a dugout, identifiable by his leather sandals and shirt, like Don Quixote in a canoe. The pilot's Sancho Panza was a barefoot lad of my own age, seemingly more interested in cadging cigarettes than learning his trade. Navigating the Delta certainly needed skills; imagine a Venetian gondolier guiding *Titanic* through a labyrinth of waterways, somehow transposed to the Amazon. To help, the rule was that the last ship in to each port was designated 'Guardship', assuming the duties of a coastal radio station. I would go on watch every four hours to advertise our position and pass any messages until a new ship arrived to relieve me. Vessels had to announce their intentions by radio, as many of the channels were too narrow for two ships to pass.

We moved up through a maze of creeks to Warri. Our anchor was dropped forward and the kedge (mini-anchor) aft in order to hold us off the bank, while we tied fast to the trees just opposite a local grass hut that was floating peacefully on a log raft in the shallows.

Imagine the occupants' alarm next morning when they found a gargantuan ship's propeller framed in their doorway – not to mention my own, waking up with my head down and feet thrust into the air. The kedge had dragged during the night till the tide left our stern high and dry, only yards from their fragile dwelling.

White Rabbits, Dark Fears

The floating bush dwelling at Warri

… and the following morning

The good news was, we could be used as a giant lure for fish. At night, I witnessed the ingenious local catching method when a net (set in a large rectangular wooden frame), was attached to the side of a dugout canoe. The outer edge of the frame was lowered deep into the water, like a hinge or scoop, while the little boat paddled sidewards.

As the net was raised, a shoal of small silvery fish avalanched straight into the bottom of the canoe. It was our ship's lights that attracted such a glistening harvest, in a unique combination of nature, tradition and modernity.

Fork and penny, beetle and snake

M.V. *Kumba* and S.S. *Carronpark* berthed at Sapele

The riskiest part of the trip came at 'The Fork' on our way up to Sapele, the furthest navigable point. This was the equivalent of manoeuvring an articulated lorry round a right angled bend on a country lane. Precise positioning was required to get the bow heading towards a specific corner of land on the port side, ready to turn hard at the apex of the t-junction. At the crucial moment, the engines were given a blast of 'full-ahead' and full rudder, urgently coaxing the stern round the 90 degree bend. But what would happen if it all went wrong? We listed to starboard as the bottom of the ship slithered over the mud. All hands assembled on deck, ready for the worst. If the pilot misjudged the turn, the crew on the fo'c'sle head would have to take cover as the bow buried itself deep in the trees on the opposite bank. Twigs brushed cheeks, scratching, scuffling and scraping till – like Houdini bursting from a straitjacket – the ship set on its new course. It's easy when you know how.

Living amid mud huts and 5,000 ton international cargo vessels, the locals also knew a thing or two. At Sapele, as we fished from the ship's side, small boys would dive from their dugouts to retrieve pennies that we threw to them. In return, they'd swim to the bottom to free our snagged fish-hooks – no mean feat in the muddy water.

Dugouts laden with fruit and veg glide down-river on the ebb

A raft of large logs at a bush berth near Sapele

The world was enchanted with teeming life, only to be cursed with hideous infestations of cockroaches that appeared in the evening in their hundreds of thousands. It was impossible to walk without killing half a dozen crunchy, two-inch-long reddish-brown beetles at every step. They crawled up the ropes and up the gangway until the ship was a seething mass. Next morning, they were magically gone.

Exploring the Niger. The author wearing the khaki shirt

White Rabbits, Dark Fears

On Sunday, we took the ship's lifeboat on an exploratory trip up some of the creeks, landing at a clearing where a group of locals took us to visit their village and turned out to pose for photographs, at our invitation. Despite their apparent remoteness from the modern world, they were entirely comfortable before the camera.

Villagers meeting our lifeboat

... and posing with some of our crew

It was us who ended up discomforted, as our ship was unable to depart at the appointed time after unwittingly loading ourselves down into the mud. Only nature could rescue us – the tide.

We proceeded to Abonema in the Eastern Delta and up the Bonny River to Port Harcourt before moving on to Calabar, where we moored midstream and discharged into barges. There was great excitement one night as the Kroo-boys set about catching two large black snakes that swam past, simply for the thrill of the hunt. My instinctive fears were as alien to them as *ju-ju* had been to my younger self.

Magical Calabar

Calabar was a small town of wood and stone buildings surrounded by a residential area of traditional mud-and-thatch houses. On top of the hill were the graves of the legendary anti-infanticide campaigner, Mary Slessor (a.k.a. 'White Queen of Calabar') along with the Orcadian nurse Margaret Graham. Much of their work was directed at protecting new-born twins, traditionally regarded as 'the devil's offspring', while also attempting to eradicate *ju-ju* acts of vengeance against those accused of black magic – a common practice in societies with pre-scientific ideas of fate and misfortune. It was here that we had a chance meeting (or was it fate?) with Mr. Somerville of the Church of Scotland Mission, so I asked if he knew a Graemsay man, Harry Mowat (Herrak o' Ramray), who had been a missionary somewhere in Africa. But of course he did. Harry had worked right there in Calabar. It was uncanny!

Passing the volcanic peak on the island of Fernando Po (now Bioko), we called at Victoria, in Cameroon, where the jungle gave way to lush grassland fringed with trees. I had to take a taxi trip through a large area of picturesque, fertile, green countryside to pay off a sick crewman at the local hospital. In times past, he might have been considered an unfortunate victim of *ju-ju* witchcraft. But no one had called for vengeance, not even a whisper. Throughout the voyage, our 'dodgy crew' had proved their mettle, as had the Kroo.

During our time in the Delta, there was some speculation about *ju-ju* but no hard evidence and no physical harm came to any of our Kroo-boys. Frequently, some of them would disappear into the jungle at night, but always returned with a song and a smiling face. We heard nothing of the human sacrifice that Captain Halcrow had witnessed. Was it all in the mind, and if so, whose minds? That was unclear, but at least Harry Mowat, along with so many others, had played a part in discouraging the practice.

Harry Mowat in his retirement

A couple of months later, I passed the pier head at home in Stromness, only to be ambushed by a presence calling after me. "Len! I had a letter from Calabar." I turned my head: "Harry!" It was magical!

8. Wild Sheep Chase

"Meester Weelson, you and I are the only two Breetish on the sheep," said Christo Petrides – or Kapetan Christo, as everyone knew him. He was a Cypriot and, as such, did indeed hold a British passport. Now he was master of the *Caspiana*, but the poor old lady had been laid up for three years and was a sorry sight, frozen in to her dock in Zeebrugge and red with rust from her mastheads to her waterline. She was a 'Liberty ship', a gift of 'Uncle Sam' during World War II, though in her current state the Germans wouldn't have wasted a bomb on her.

At your convenience

Although Greek-owned, she was registered in Liberia. At the time, most countries avoided so-called 'flags of convenience' like a bubonic outbreak as they were seen as lowering of standards and a disloyalty to the home country. But the Greeks had no such qualms, attracted by the lack of regulation and low taxes afforded by listing their ships in 'dodgy' locations like Panama and, of course, Liberia.

Money talks, and as they were dangling a golden fleece (tax free) right there in front of us, who was I to refuse? Some companies were paying up to £100 per month, but Goulandris Brothers offered £70 which I found attractive enough, joining at their London office in January 1960.

S.S. *Caspiana* in Emden. Radio callsign ELCA
A 'Sam Boat' Liberty ship built in America. 7,000 g.r.t.

On British ships I was 'Sparks', but now, with the Greeks, I was 'Marconi', though I was usually honoured with the title 'Meester Weelson'.

The author in the radio cabin of *Caspiana*

Our flag of convenience brought few actual conveniences – that was for the owners – so we had no heating on board, despite a temperature well below freezing. The engineers got the generators started and were working on the hot water, but when I stepped out of my bunk, I found myself splashing about ankle-deep in a freezing pool. Days of toil got the engines turning before we moved to dry-dock in Rotterdam for a week cleaning and anti-fouling the bottom. Convenient, it was not. Then it was through the Kiel Canal in Germany to Gdynia (Poland) to load coal for Karachi. The harbour in Gdynia had four inches of ice with a foot of snow on the ground, but we still ended up smeared in a thin coat of black soot.

Going ashore, Thanasis (the third mate) and I got a resounding reprimand from a uniformed gold-braided 'admiral' for not keeping on the invisible pavement. Post-war Poland was that kind of place: bossy, bleak and bare shelved. In a bar one night, an important looking man entered. "Pssst," the barmaid hissed, "he's a Communist." Evidently, some people were more equal than others in the workers' paradise. To prove it, Kapetan Christo, the chief engineer and myself were invited to visit an establishment that was not open to the public. The house of ill-repute was discreetly located in a warehouse, ushering us into an eye-popping panorama of beauties, all laid tantalising out before us. We hesitated. For the right price we could have the most desired and lusted after goods in Eastern Europe, top of the range, precisely labelled in American dollars. The chief couldn't resist, grabbing himself a short wave radio, though I ended up repairing it after a few weeks of use. So much for luxury communism!

All Greek

I soon learned, under flags of convenience, normal shipping rules did not apply. Only three officers held certificates of rank: the captain, chief engineer and myself. But qualifications were apparently a slippery thing. The mate, Josef Constantinidi, in fact, held a second mate's ticket (or certificate), whereas second mate, Eraklis Paolis was, actually, an able seaman. And when he departed in Port Said, a 'mere' bosun got his job. And the third mate, Thanasis Dimitriou, was a senior apprentice, but when he also left in Egypt, a young first tripper (who was, entirely coincidentally, the nephew of the skipper's wife) naturally took his place. Very convenient.

For even extra convenience, Thanasis determined that I should learn Greek. By the time he left in Port Said, I had a fair vocabulary of useful phrases – some not for polite company! Years later, when on holiday in Crete, a local man working in his vegetable patch addressed me. "No speak English. You speak Greek?" My fruity reply, *"Ligo, ligo. Kitta tin kolotripida sou!"* convulsed him in so much laughter, I thought he'd have a seizure. He was still laughing as we walked back half an hour later. A delicate translation would be: "Consult your rear end before you talk to me!"

We also had two ladies on board, the skipper's wife, Giota, and the chief engineer's, Louiza. Giota was encouraged to converse with me to improve her English, though the company's engineering superintendent in Rotterdam, an Englishman, was horrified that she would talk with a Scottish accent. On the other hand, our steward, Costa Constantinos, didn't speak a word of English, but we discovered we both had school French, which I never imagined would be useful. By the end of the voyage, we conversed in a strange mixture of Greek, English and Français.

Angry Neptune

Soon, we were to be tested. A stiff wind was getting up when the steering gear packed in, just off the coast of Holland. Our liberty ship was suddenly liberated from the commander's control in one of the world's busiest shipping lanes for a tense ten minutes before the emergency wheel was brought into use. Not before time. Passing Brittany, we were now in a full south-westerly gale which, by Biscay, was an even fuller force 10, ratcheting up to force 12 by Cape Finisterre, the north-west tip of Spain. For three more days we pressed on at 3 knots, head to wind, as our nose bored deep into gigantic green breakers, avalanching down the fore-deck with enormous force against the front of our centre-castle, shuddering like medieval ramparts. The slow-motion stresses on the ship's hull were only just countered by our cargo of coal, pounded relentlessly by the elemental forces. Liberty ships were known to break in two in such conditions, but Kapetan Christo stayed on the bridge, keeping a Breetish stiff upper lip – while we all prayed in a mixture of Greek, English and French.

Angry Neptune did eventually relent: we had apparently passed the test with flying or at least 'convenient' colours. But now we were lost. I had to take a number of radio bearings from the Portuguese beacons to fix our position so we could set course for Gibraltar, then onwards through the Med to Port Said (Egypt). Thankfully, the weather rewarded us with some calm and warmth, so the 'crowd' set about our rust with chipping hammers like a thousand masseurs and hairdressers. The old girl had earned a makeover and a bit of 'tender loving care' to get her all dolled up and ready for action.

But I spoke too soon. As we queued for the canal, the Suez pilot refused to move us when the rudder indicator in the wheelhouse refused to work. It was not my responsibility, but with a bit of intuition and 'mither wit', I got it going in about 20 minutes and we were on our way, straight into a sandstorm. The portholes had to be kept closed, but the fine grains still found their way in – to mix with the soot and rust.

Yum-yum

On arrival at Karachi (West Pakistan), it seemed they were in no hurry. No hurry at all. It would be another ten whole days before they even found us a berth, very much at their own convenience. As we lay at anchor, fishing became the main pastime, even if there was little to catch. The ladies got quite excited one night when Giota caught a rather small puffer fish.

The local fishermen, in their lateen-sail outrigger canoes, really

Georgiou, Kapetan Christo, Giota and Louiza with their 'catch of the day'

knew how to do it (and where to sell too), heading for all the 'convenience' ships with their catches. Our skipper bought as much as he could every day, paying with cigarettes – fags for fish. Greeks certainly did not waste food, so somebody always ended up with the head on his plate with the eyeballs to suck. Yum-yum!

Midnight, every Greek ship – and they were numerous – blasted their sirens in cacophonous unison, apparently heralding World War III. In fact, it was Easter, the biggest, most joyous Orthodox festival. Our whole ship's company squeezed into the officers' saloon for a nocturnal feast, including moussaka, of course, plus the one and only dessert of the whole voyage – and some *vino*. Our old rust bucket surely rivalled the *Queen Mary* that one and only miraculous day.

Sadly, unloading in Karachi was painfully disorganised. The city itself was an enticing maze of fascinating side streets, full of artisan

Wild Sheep Chase

A common mode of transport in Karachi

workshops, but large parts were strictly no-go areas for foreigners. We typically got turned back by an army officer as we entered a dodgy street. Yet, we dined at a swanky hotel where an orchestra entertained the rather well-to-do westernised clientèle. It was a world of haves and have-nots, policed by a thin line of moustachioed military.

It was time to go. Our poor old ship had sailed out soot black, but we would return red rouge, after loading iron ore at Marmagoa (Portuguese India) which, in fact, left us steaming precariously overloaded back through the canal and into the Mediterranean. "Meester Weelson … a sheep, a sheep!" barked the captain as we neared Gibraltar, heavily laden in ominous darkness. Most inconveniently, no one on the bridge could manage Morse code, so I had to flash the Aldis lamp. The 'sheep' was certainly not one you'd want to ram you. Dappled in the moonlight, I gazed at an overwhelming and rapidly approaching silhouette, its eye blinking … *dit dah, dit dah, dit dah*. I translated rapidly: "British warship *Victorious*," asking "what ship?" Royal Navy signallers are reputed to be pretty nifty at Morse, so I tested him with a torrent of dashes and dots, just to show them what 'convenience' sheeps could do. He got the message: our redoubtable aircraft carrier signed off with the customary 'BV' – ('*Bon Voyage*').

Ticketless sheep, qualified goats

In sight of home, an equally abrupt message arrived from the owners. A rule change: uncertificated men would now have to sit a Liberian exam. What?! The problem was, we had too many ticketless sheep and not enough qualified goats. There was no choice: we would dodge the whole thing by transferring to the Greek flag when we got to Emden (Germany). A wailing chorus cried out – no more tax-free salaries! "But you will be OK, Meester Weelson," reassured Kapetan Christo. "I will tell them you are paying Breetish tax." Most convenient.

Just to wipe the smile off, a final inconvenience arrived in the post. A rat-eyed official had noted my lack of British-registered seagoing activities; I would therefore be liable for National Service call-up. This was it: the dreaded draft.

My pursuit of the golden (tax free) fleece had come to an end. *"Kitta tin kolotripida sou!"*

9. Over and Out

Longfellow was preparing to meet Robbie Burns, behind the Iron Curtain. The Anglo-Danubian Shipping Company of London owned five vessels, all named after poets and writers: *Thackeray, Tennyson,* etc. We'd need their communicative flair where we were going.

M.V. *Longfellow*. Radio callsign MQQN
Built by Henry Robb, Leith. 3948 g.r.t.

Red faces

In July 1960, we were deep in the Cold War – the time of Sputnik, James Bond and Checkpoint Charlie. Despite threats of mutually assured destruction, Armageddon, etc., trade actually continued, so we were bound for Murmansk in Arctic Russia to pick up a cargo of timber for Leith, under a mainly British crew with greasers from the Yemen. Our solitary Latvian able seaman, fearing abduction in the USSR, wisely opted to wait for our return. It was that kind of time.

It was also a time for the seaman's favourite – rum. The company provided a half-bottle for every Sunday we spent at sea. Where we were going, we might well need it. It was to be shared between the mates and myself, but two of them were tee-total, so the second mate and I looked forward to happy weekends. But would we get to enjoy them? On departure, the skipper gave me a message for the agency in Moscow containing the details of our voyage, but that summer we suffered an intense period of high sunspot activity which disturbs the ionosphere, making short wave communication extremely difficult.

Murmansk, in the Kola Inlet

Over and Out

So, I was not immediately able to make contact with any Russian radio station. Perhaps I should have sensed an omen, but internationally recognised procedure required I send the message to Portishead Radio for onward transmission by landline to Moscow. I hoped for the best.

Permanent daylight with permanent sunshine greeted us north of the Arctic Circle. As we rounded Norway, I could hear the Murmansk coastal radio station loud and clear, so gave him a call. 'UMV UMV UMV de MQQN'... but no reply. I persisted... and again. Even within sight of the station, there was nothing. It was odd. Our equipment was working fine. They must have been under instruction not to communicate with foreigners, I concluded. The Old Man was informed, but he had no option but to continue to the pilot station at the entrance to the Kola Inlet, still 26 miles from Murmansk harbour.

We lay there for an hour, drumming our fingers. There was no sign of life, neither on shore nor afloat. All dead. UMV was silent. So we sailed on regardless: a British cargo vessel flying the 'red duster' in full, blatant view of the Northern Fleet of the Soviet Union – and they didn't even notice. James Bond never had it this easy!

We'd already reached the inner station. After another hour, the skipper decided to proceed without a pilot, though Murmansk was still not visible as it lay round a bend about 15 miles ahead. The response came without warning: a fast launch sliced through the waves like a harpoon targeting a whale. Half a dozen menacing officers, weighed down with gold braid, climbed our boarding ladder demanding to know what we were doing. They peered at our papers suspiciously, till the truth dawned. No message had reached from Moscow. It was red faces – or worse – for the Red Fleet.

Back in the USSR

"We need to see your papers" was enough to send an Arctic chill down any spine, even in an emergency. A West German ship, homeward bound from Arkhangel diverted into Murmansk with a large deck-cargo of timber that had shifted, giving her an alarming list to port. She looked as though she might capsize at any moment. The crew dropped anchor in the harbour and abandoned ship – just in the nick of time for she was soon lying on her side, barely peeping above the surface. At the German captain's request our skipper went to visit them ashore, returning with copies of the vessel's papers, just in case the Russians confiscated his originals. You never really knew.

But that wasn't all. The skipper's 16-year-old son, Claus, was on his school holidays accompanying his Dad for a bit of adventure. He certainly got it – he was the only one to return home, leaving all of his shipmates back in the USSR.

The ad is mightier ...

In the event our hosts also hugged us pretty close. We were well catered for at the Murmansk Seamans Club, no doubt so they could keep an eye on us, while displaying the clear superiority of the Soviet socialist system. The television showed endless film of farm workers slaving their guts out in the fields to the accompaniment of rousing patriotic music, while a display board was proudly plastered with photos of the captured American pilot Gary Powers beside the wreckage of his U2 spy plane shot down only two months earlier. To cap it all, they were also selling Robbie Burns bicentenary stamps. The poet Longfellow never received such a foreign honour but Scotland's national bard was deemed sufficiently radical to be toasted by the heirs of Lenin, unlike the British Post Office.

Meanwhile, we were deemed sufficiently important to have a bus tour of the city and surrounding area. We were free to roam around, but tailed by a couple of KGB men following at a discrete distance. The club even laid on a dance one night, but none of the girls spoke English. The jovial English-speaking Russian who joined us for a drink every night was, of course, planted too. He expressed an interest

Claus and third mate, Mr. Jones, in Leith Docks

in western reading material, so our second engineer collected some *Reader's Digest* magazines for him. The security man at the dock gates called him over and examined the books. Without a word of English, he went through page after page and ripped out, not the bourgeois Yankee propaganda, but every coloured advert showing Ford, Kodak, Hilton, Chanel, Levis, Coca Cola ... Evidently, a picture bellowed a thousand words, while Burns was nary a threat ... although as a wise man once put it: "Suspicion is a heavy armour and with its weight it impedes more than it protects." (attr. Burns)

We sailed a week later, with a pilot on board, taking young Claus en route to Leith for an unscheduled tour of Edinburgh. Meanwhile, I was back on air to advise of our departure: UMV UMV UMV de MQQN MQQN MQQN TR ... Silence.

Hail the sporting youth

After escaping the KGB on the way back to Leith, I ended up in a bar with the Führer's finest in Wilhelmshaven, our next destination. Not so youthful by this time, a retired skipper (German of course) proudly told me how he had commanded a square rigged sail-training ship before the war. He showed me a photo, and there she was, berthed in Cape Town with Table Mountain in the background, boldly flying the swastika. Obviously, one of the Hitler Youth training vessels.

But people change, especially the young, shaped and moulded by their surroundings. We had a young deck-boy by the name of Tanbini, obviously of Italian extraction, with parents who had an ice-cream shop in Dundee in Scotland. He didn't speak his parents' language, but the dockers in Genoa, our next port of call, couldn't believe it. On his brief stay, he had more of his legs pulled than a centipede on a torturer's rack – in Italian, of course.

Nearby in Savona, a pastel-shaded port on the Italian Riviera, we came across a dockside bar with a band and young singer performing every night, including a Spanish seaman with an impressive voice who specialised in, *'I'll give him a bunion on his Spanish onion if I catch him bending tonight'* – sung, of course, in melodious Español. Better still was his ship: the S.S. *Nuestra Senora del Carmen* – probably the last turret-deck ship afloat. Close to 200 were built by Doxford on

A turret ship in the Suez Canal
(Australian War Memorial)

the river Wear in the late 19th/early 20th century, as the Suez Canal dues used to be calculated on the ship's beam at deck level. To cut the cost of transit, Doxford designed a vessel with a wide hull and narrow deck. So, we might note that ships were also moulded by their surroundings, though the result looked like a boat squeezed into an Edwardian corset.

We arrived at the singer's homeland, Franco's dictatorship, and headed for the country's most stereotypical icon: Barcelona's bullring. During the performance, we all got carried away with the excitement of the crowd, but it was a cruel affair with nothing sporting about it – rather like the regime. The poor old bull was tormented and wounded to the point of exhaustion before the young 'victorious' matador finished him off with a single thrust of his sword.

The bullfight in Barcelona

Longer strides

After nearly five months, we were getting weary too as our vessel zigzagged from port to port before heading for St. John, New Brunswick, in the Bay of Fundy, way over the Atlantic on the Canadian coast.
It was thoroughly disorienting experience. Were we going crazy? We'd go ashore climbing up the gangway and come back on board *still* climbing up – the rise and fall of the tide was close to 40 feet. Even stranger, at the mouth of the St. John river, the gargling rapids of the Reversing Falls flowed backwards, driven by the power of flood tide – as uncanny as any *ju-ju* magic.

Summerside, a small town on the south coast of Prince Edward Island, was uncanny too. The island was 'dry' at that time, but we hadn't been tied up half an hour before we knew the address of the

New Brunswick, Nova Scotia and Prince Edward Island

nearest bootlegger. A crowd of men sat all round the four walls of the room, yarning and downing beer. One, who lived on his own on the edge of town, treated us to a delicious plate of salmon smolts that he'd caught earlier that day. His granny was from the Highlands and spoke Gaelic but, although he was friendly to a fault, he insisted on telling the corniest story about a tight-fisted Scotsman.

> Old McTavish, a Highlander, had just bought his young son his first pair of leather boots. They were strictly for Sunday wear only, so he ran barefoot the rest of the week. The lad couldn't wait for the day when he proudly stepped out in his brand new, freshly polished footwear as the family walked to church. But it wasn't long before his father was glowering at the boy's feet. "Is there something wrong with my boots, Dad?" the boy whispered. "No son – nothing wrong with the boots – just take longer strides!"

At last

Maybe you had to be there. But as it turned out, it was I who was going to take longer strides. Aboard again, we gazed up at nature's Hollywood spectacular, the aurora borealis, just off Newfoundland, before suffering nature's tantrums back in the Med, tossing us about like a washing machine. We nipped into port, brushing past the brutalities of the conflict in Algeria (buzzed daily by swarms of helicopters as the war of independence reached its climax). And just as abruptly, we were home for Christmas, at last.

Seafaring was a great adventure for the young and unattached, but when they had a wife and children, they longed for a stable life. There was always someone on board moaning: "This is my last trip. I'm getting a shore job when we pay off." But sure enough, they'd turn up again for another 'last trip', ready for yet another spin in the washing machine. Of course, a youthful sort like me had no intention of leaving the sea, but on the train north, I met up with someone who told me of a businessman who might be interested in employing me. I went for interview; got the job. All of a sudden, that was it. A family history of centuries at sea – over and out! Almost …

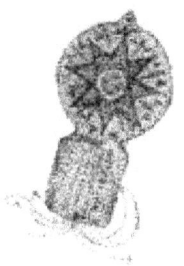

10. Latter-day Vikings

The red-heads exploded over the known (and often the unknown) world, plunging across seas and waterways, from Greenland to Galway, Kirkwall to Kiev. Population pressure, macho greed, technological edge, climate pressure – or all of the above – seem to have energised them with a warrior lust for life (and death). But it was their blond, and not so blond, ancestors that settled and sailed again, down through the ages, as did mine – as did I. Ultimately, these were the people who set me on my voyages, with their salt-bleached characters lying hidden among the tentacles and tendrils of my entangled ancestry, swaying like seaweed in the tides of time.

Thrashing tails

On clippers and barques, they sailed the world, trading around the globe and – for the tougher lads – up to the crimson seas and thrashing tails of the oil-rich Arctic (whale oil, of course). It was hazardous – whaling especially so. Forby Sutherland wasn't the only one lost in his prime. In 1836, the *Advice*, the *Thomas* and the *Dee* arrived back from Baffin Bay (Canada), with the loss of more than a hundred men. The danger wasn't a deterrent though. The excitement of the chase and a pot of cash at the end, drove them on. As a mere 16-year-old, great grandfather James Wilson made his first trip to the Davis

Straits in 1867, hugging close to Greenland on the famous old whaler, *Truelove* of Hull, (captured from the Americans during the War of Independence).

Congealed seas

The Hull whaler *Truelove* built in Philadelphia in 1761
(Hull Museum)

Whether for true love or not, James set off again the following year together with his brother Bill and their cousin, James Skinner. They surely wouldn't have got life insurance. On this occasion, they survived the wreck of the *Wildfire* of Dundee in the northern reaches of Baffin Bay, but their skipper, Captain Walker, was ashen-faced:

… we were six of the finest vessels that ever navigated these congealed seas, lying close together to be shoved up at the mercy of the immense floes. We […] could do nothing but look on, expecting every moment to see our ships made mincemeat of. (Norman Watson, *The Dundee Whalers* p. 24.)

It was Bill Wilson's second Arctic misadventure, for he was a 19-year-old seaman on the whaler *Emma* when she sprang a leak and sank in frigid waters, just to the east of Greenland in 1864. Eventually, the brothers moved to the North Atlantic run, carrying passengers and cargo from the Clyde to eastern Canada. Whaling was a young man's – or sometimes, a dead man's – game.

Above:
James Wilson

Left:
Bill Wilson

Despite the risks, Orcadians were inveterate globetrotters following in the footsteps of their Viking ancestors. Some stayed closer: Magnus Lyon got his master's ticket in Liverpool in 1851 and from 1856 he commanded the paddle steamer *Royal Mail*, the first steamship to serve on the stomach-churning Pentland Firth between Stromness and the Scottish mainland. Meanwhile, at the other end of the world, Captain Daniel Sutherland served as a 22-year-old able seaman in

Australian waters in 1870 before getting his master's ticket. His mother was of the Lyon family and when he married a cousin, Jane Sutherland, they moved to live in North Shields on the Tyne – but he never let "auld acquaintance be forgot". On his way to America in 1896, he paid a surprise visit to his home island, as reported in the *Orkney Herald* newspaper, no less:

> The S.S. *Isle of Kent*, Capt. Sutherland, passed through Hoy Sound on Sunday evening last, and came to anchor off the island of Graemsay for a few hours where the friends and relatives of the captain and other members of the crew had an opportunity of boarding the vessel and renewing old acquaintanceship.

Captain Daniel Sutherland with his daughter and her husband

Sixpence for a favourable wind

Stromness was like a motorway service station. Eighteenth century European conflicts made the English Channel a risky place to be, so ships of all nationalities preferred to take the northern route round

Latter-day Vikings

Britain. With a sheltered harbour, the little town grew to become a pit-stop where ship-masters could pick up provisions and crewmen and wait for suitable conditions to carry them safely westwards. Bessie-Millie, the witch of Brinkie's Brae, charged sixpence for a favourable wind. What more could a ship-master want?

Pit stops, of course, needed 'mechanics' and the demands of island life ensured that Orcadians could supply an abundant number of them, spanning the globe as they went. As youngsters, they became skilled at many crafts, notably house and boat-building, while the women did the spinning and knitting, tended the hens (and the pig) to put food on the table – not to mention altering the wind direction for a price.

It was the Ritch family that dominated our line's seafaring experience from the latter half of the 19th century. Great grandfather, George Ritch, served his apprenticeship as a shipwright with Stanger in Stromness and subsequently led a rip-roaring life at sea, all of it as a carpenter in sail, while his wife and family tended their small croft, aptly named Windywalls. Like their Viking forebears, they kept one foot at home and one abroad as they tilled, toiled and travelled.

Great grandparents Mary (Sinclair) and George Ritch c. 1908

Barques, Sparks & Sharks

George and Mary's home, Windywalls,
with their granddaughter Cathie in the kailyard

On a mission

These latter-day Norsemen also brought their own god with them. Thor and Odin were long abandoned when George sailed with the Moravian Mission (a religious organisation based in Germany). With the encouragement of a British Government anxious to improve relationships with the Inuit, they established a network of mission stations all along the coast of Labrador and serviced them annually with a ship optimistically named the *Harmony*. Stromness was the last port of departure for their annual voyage carrying a supply of the Industrial Revolution's finest manufactures before returning to London with purest sealskin and oil. George over-wintered in Labrador building a schooner for the Mission.

A proper cuppa

But the quest for profit – quick profit – drove constant waves of manic innovation to deliver, above all, a proper cuppa. British ships were built for maximum cargo-carrying capacity, making them cumbersome and slow, but when the fast American ship *Oriental* had the audacity to compete successfully on the China to London tea run in 1850, the gloves came off. The result was ultra-streamlined sailing ships with a massive spread of sail. The tea clipper was born – the Formula 1 racer of its day. The refinement of its design was driven by an annual 'tea race', with a big prize for the first ship home each season. In turn, it was made almost obsolete by the opening of the Suez Canal in 1869 and the introduction of steam engines, forcing the clippers to search for trade elsewhere, in every corner of the globe. It was a ruthless age. The men, of course, followed the ships. George Ritch and his sons sailed the oceans for all their working lives. Arriving young in Australia, George actually left his vessel to try his hand at gold-mining, eventually bringing home a nugget – one solitary lump – but even it got lost after his son Hughie died. Like nature's casino, the Gold Rush saw more losers than winners.

Ritch in name

With no luck and no gold, George was Ritch in name only, instead becoming rich in offspring. Children followed, one after the other, after he married Mary Sinclair of Scarateen, who dutifully produced no less than 13: nine sons and four daughters. One girl died in childhood, another as a teenager and two sons perished at sea in their early 20s. A 19th century life was full of death. Yet, opportunities beckoned: seven of their sons and eight of their grandsons served at sea. Three sons married three of the Sutherland sisters, resulting in a large close-knit extended family where most of the menfolk were seafarers. With a growing population, Orcadians were driven like their Viking forefathers to scour the seas.

Barques, Sparks & Sharks

In 1864, aged 25, George served in the Australian wool trade as carpenter on the clipper *Centurion* of Aberdeen
(Watercolour by D. H. L. Little. State Library of Victoria)

William and Mary Ritch

Hereditary, incestuous, nepotistic?

It's hard to keep count as generation begat generation. Grandfather William Ritch, husband of Mary Sutherland, went to the herring fishing before becoming a farmer-fisherman. Six of his brothers, six nephews, plus his son George, his sons-in-law and several brothers-in-law, sailed the wider oceans. All together, six master mariners, eight carpenters, four seamen and one engineer. The oldest brother, James, followed in his father's footsteps to Labrador as carpenter on the *Harmony*, now commanded by a fellow Graemsay man, Henry Linklater, who was a nephew by marriage of the previous skipper, Captain White. It was virtually hereditary, suspiciously incestuous – almost nepotistic. Henry's brother John (Hurricane Jeck), for instance, sailed as first mate and, on Henry's retiral, succeeded him as master and their cousin Joseph was master of the Mission ships *Cordelia* and *Gleaner*.

The Mission ship
Harmony

Captain Henry Linklater

'Hurricane Jeck' Linklater

George and Mary's son James Ritch, 1890s
He rounded Cape Horn 27 times – 12 under sail and 15 in steam.

After one trip to Labrador, James Ritch moved to warmer climes on square-riggers including the *Cromdale, City of Delhi* and *City of Florence,* dodging in and out of steamships in the 1890s, before settling in the Port Line.

Cromdale

Through the hawse-pipe

Life was a jostling hierarchy. It's clear the family was determinedly upwardly-mobile, sometimes doing it the hard way. James's sons, James Jnr, John and William continued the seafaring tradition (two carpenters and one seaman), but even though James senior's other siblings, George-Robert, Charlie and Magnus, didn't have the benefit of apprenticeships, they rose by merit 'through the hawse-pipe' (literally the conduit for the anchor chain) to eventually serve as officers on the after-deck.

But you never knew. Two of George and Mary's sons perished at sea, John of tuberculosis on board the Aberdeen clipper *Patriarch* in 1893, aged only 23, thousands of miles from home in the Indian Ocean. Isaac lost his life even younger when the four-masted full-rigger *County of Selkirk* disappeared without trace on the homeward run from Calcutta in 1896. His brother, George-Robert, met him on the eve of the fateful voyage and was probably on the *County of Aberdeen* that sailed the following day. Little wonder sailors were superstitious.

Latter-day Vikings

Patriarch

County of Selkirk

Barques, Sparks & Sharks

Despite the carnage, Orcadians continued to thrust themselves into the modernising industrial world. This was the 'real' Gold Rush of the 19th century. When brothers George, Charlie and Magnus got their master's tickets, they rose to become aristocrats of steam, serving with immediate promotion as skippers in the King Line Shipping Company. George on the *King David* in 1895, followed by Charlie on the *King Bleddyn* in 1898 and the youngest, Magnus, on the *King David* in 1905 – by which time, George had also moved to the *King Bleddyn* and Charlie to the *King Gruffydd*. It was a leapfrogging game of chess.

Like his father and older brother James, George Jnr. started his career on the mission ships sailing to Labrador. By 1888, aged 20, he was an able seaman on the *Brilliant* on the Australia run, and seven years later he had a command of his own, the S.S. *King David*.

Above: *Brilliant* of Aberdeen

Left: George-Robert Ritch. A man of short stature but a commanding presence. His nephew, Isaac Wilson, referred to him as 'The Admiral'

Latter-day Vikings

The same Captain George Ritch as Marine Superintendent of the King Line, with his wife Lizzie Linklater, daughter of John 'Hurricane Jeck' Linklater

Wheel's Kick and the Wind's Song

Coriolanus
(State Library of South Australia)

Time was money. As modernity whipped the world into a faster spin, seafarers had to be speedsters. As an engineering marvel, the iron-hulled clipper *Coriolanus* was one of the finest ships of her day, though not for the faint-hearted. In February 1890, the steamer *Claymore* crossed her path about 400 miles west of the Fastnet lighthouse. In the resulting collision, the *Claymore* sank, but the *Coriolanus* survived. After repairs, she sailed for Australia in the summer of the same year with George Ritch as her 22-year-old second mate, proud of leaving rivals in its wake, if not on the seabed. In his book *The Wheel's Kick and the Wind's Song*, Captain A. G. Course quotes George's recollection of the voyage.

> The *Coriolanus* was to me a very easy 16 to 17 knot ship ... During both outward and homeward we met many ships, but we never passed or found any that could keep company with us for any length of time.

Oil, wine and water

Competing empires stampeded to the edge. Seafaring was already hazardous enough, but World War I only increased the dangers – notably submarines, the sharks of the seas. In December of 1916, George lost the *King Bleddyn* to a surface attack by the German U-boat UC21, 30 miles off the coast of Brittany. He evacuated and was taken on board the submarine where he and the U-boat commander recognised each other from a pre-war encounter. Chivalry was not yet dead. A 'celebratory' bottle of wine was opened and he was given a course to steer for a safe landing. Commander Reinhold Saltzwedel of the U-boat wasn't so lucky as he died in September 1917 when UB81 struck a mine in the English Channel.

George suffered yet another loss in September 1918, with the *War Arabis* in the Western Mediterranean when she was torpedoed by U34 en-route to Marseilles, only two months before the end of the war. The commander of this U-boat was, in turn, lost with all hands the following month. By this point, the hunters were increasingly the hunted.

But George was virtually unstoppable. He rose to be the company commodore and eventually their first marine superintendent. Likewise, his son, Jack, followed suit as skipper and commodore of the King Line, though his ship also was torpedoed during World War II. At the other end of the scale, Jack's brother, George Jnr., served down in the engine room, much to his father's displeasure. For the self-made men of the seas, 'oil and water don't mix!'

The gentleman and the bruiser

The mustachioed gentleman of the Ritch brothers was Charlie. He served as a 22-year-old able seaman on the *Old Kensington* in 1890/91, getting his master's ticket and command of the King Line steamer *King Bleddyn* in 1898. Unscathed in the war, his career was not incident-free, with two collisions and three groundings. Manoeuvrability and navigation aids were not to today's standard, as Hollywood's worst disaster epics remind us.

Old Kensington

Barques, Sparks & Sharks

Captain Charlie Ritch with his dog and some of his men on the S.S. *Don Cesar* c.1905. The ship belonged to the Buenos Aires & Pacific Railway Co. and was managed by the King Line

Charlie Ritch (R) with a visitor, Captain Scarth of Binscarth, Orkney, on board *King Frederick* in Portland Oregon, 1923

Captain Magnus Ritch in his tropical going-ashore suit

With a Viking name and an axe-wielding spirit, Captain Magnus Ritch, was from a very different mould. Like his brothers, he started as an ordinary seaman in sail, but he built himself a reputation as a boxer with a fondness for his beer who stood no nonsense. A King Line veteran once told me his legendary drinking had come to the notice of the board of directors. But they didn't sack him. An exceptional skipper, he stoutly defended the company's interests. A tough guy, perhaps, but '*our* tough guy'.

Proving the point, Captain John Allan of Stromness, who sailed with Magnus, relates 'The Hooghly Incident', about the British pilots on the river leading up to Calcutta.

They were very posh and self-important and came on board complete with a native servant-man in tow. On this occasion, the pilot ... must have been offensive as Magnus didn't grace him with a reply. He just raised his fist and floored him ... a sacking offence

Magnus commanded S.S. *Don Benito* on the Buenos Aires run from 1906 to 1912

He still kept his job, though. Clearly, he was a survivor even when, like his brothers, he suffered his share of collisions and groundings. The most serious was in 1912, when the *Don Benito* was run down by none other than Rear-Admiral Cradock's flagship, H.M.S. *London*, during fog in the English Channel. The *Benito* was seriously holed below the waterline and was lucky to survive. On Saturday 18th May, 1912, the *Orcadian* newspaper reported the 'remarkable escape' as if rivalling the *Titanic*.

> The *London*'s engines had been stopped ten minutes [...] otherwise the ram of the warship, which is a ship of 15,000 tons displacement, must have cut the railway steamer in two [...] After the collision occurred the steamer's boats were swung out and lifebelts made ready, as water was rushing into the hold. The master of the *Don Benito* is Capt. Magnus Ritch, a native of Graemsay and at the time of the accident [...] his wife and child were on board.

Latter-day Vikings

The ship's officers and apprentices pictured before the collision
(Magnus with his daughter Agnes and her mother Kitty)

His escapology held even during the war when his ship, S.S. *Boldwell*, was torpedoed about 60 miles west of Malta in 1917, going down with the loss of three men. But his career was finally scuttled after what Captain John Allan has called 'The Panama Canal Incident' when Magnus's vessel, *Cape Corso*, collided with and sank the Colon pilot boat. Although exonerated in this case, the verdict following his slurred, red-faced report at Head Office was clear – one too many refreshments en-route. It was over. An inglorious slip after a rich and rewarding 48-year rise up the 'hawse-pipe'.

Iron cracks

Tough lives forged iron character, but each had their breaking point. My father's uncle, James Ritch, for instance, worked in the Port Line, where Captain Linklater from Stromness was Marine Superintendent, until something suddenly snapped. The mate from his ship told of James's metallic temperament, leading to an abrupt exit.

> ... after Captain Linklater retired, the new Superintendent paid a visit. When he spotted an open manhole on the deck he turned to James and ordered him to, "Get that cover back on!" James squared up, looking him straight in the eye, and replied, quietly but firmly, "The man who took it off can put it back on!"

Like his brother, Captain Magnus Ritch, his seagoing career terminated that instant, but he had kept his dignity in the face of bullying hierarchies. He returned to Stromness where he continued to work, ever practical, on his own account as a boatbuilder.

The last

Quiet, experienced, iron-souled toilers, builders and sometimes boozers – we have seen how, for generations, Orcadians had proven themselves as latter-day Viking globalisers, traders and craftsmen with a taste for risky adventure. For better and for worse, my family was in the thick of it. Yet, times were a-changing fast. Empires were ebbing, technologies transforming. The dominated were learning from the dominant. By my 20s, the age of the container ship was nigh. The world had become flat (or flatter), with a more level playing field for new market entrants (Asians and others), ready to leapfrog their way into global trade.

The writing was on the wall for 'sparks' too. Maritime Satellite Communication started its development in the 1970s and the last 'dit' was sent from a UK coastal radio station on the 1st of January 1998. By then I'd switched, keeping ships of the skies afloat the rest of my career as an air traffic engineer, installing and maintaining communication and air navigation ground services – like a 'sparks' of the stratosphere – still keeping 'em safe'. An era was over, as a new one dawned, leaving shadows of barques (and sharks) flickering in memories and half-hidden legacies. I would be the last to head for the sea.

Appendix: The Fallen

History is a graveyard. Many more relatives followed the seagoing life and, sadly, too many of them died prematurely, mostly in distant places:

- Seaman John Ritch of The Netherhoose suffered a fatal accident in 1851. He is buried in St. Hilda's cemetery in Hartlepool, County Durham.

Erected in memory of
JOHN RITCH
who lost his life on Board of the
DIADAM of HARTLEPOOL
By falling from the maintop into the
Hold on the 20th of February 1851
Aged 45 Years
The above was a Native of Stromness
Orkney North Britain

Barques, Sparks & Sharks

• Great grandmother Mary Ritch's brother, James Sinclair of Scarateen, was a 19-year-old seaman just returned from a voyage to New York in September of 1858 when he and his cousins Joseph and Catherine Lyon perished in Hoy Sound. Their boat was swamped by a heavy squall as they left Stromness Harbour.

• Captain John Sutherland died in the West Indies in 1862 aged 38.

• James Linklater died in Cardiff in 1864 aged 17.

• Joseph Mowat Jnr, son of Captain Joseph Mowat and Margaret Ritch, died in 1866, aged 25, whilst rescuing passengers from the Western Ocean Packet *Albion* aground on the Point o' Ree in Graemsay. His name is engraved on the RNLI memorial in Poole, Dorset.

• James Lyon died in Santos, Brazil, on board the S.S. *John Williamson* in 1874, aged 27.

• Captain Henry Sutherland of the full-rigged ship *Canute* died in Mobile, Alabama in 1885, aged 60.

• Father's uncle, John Ritch, died of tuberculosis and was buried at sea in the Indian Ocean in 1893, aged 23.

• John's brother, Isaac, lost his life in 1896, aged 22, when his ship, the *County of Selkirk*, disappeared without trace in the Indian Ocean.

• George Sinclair, another brother of Mary Ritch, survived a shipwreck in the north of Labrador. When he married Isabella Mowat of Gorn, they emigrated to Oregon to be farmers and he died in 1899, aged 55, when his horses bolted and he fell foul of the wagon wheels.

Appendix: The Fallen

George and Isabella Sinclair with their children George, Margaret, John, Domima, Eliza, James and Robert

• John George Linklater died in Mobile, Alabama, in 1900. He was 15 and on his first trip to sea when he was struck by the anchor chain on board the *King David*. The master was his neighbour, relative and mentor, Captain George Ritch.

• Joseph Linklater, a son of Captain Joseph Linklater of the Moravian Mission ships, was third mate on S.S. *Nemesis* when she was lost with all hands off the Australian coast in 1904.

• Captain James Sinclair of The Netherhoose died in Fremantle in 1905 aged 60. Following a failed business venture in Samoa, he settled in Western Australia where he managed a goldmine in Coolgardie. His business partner wrote to say he died of a brain haemorrhage but an Australian newspaper reported his death as murder.

• Isaac Mowat, a seaman from Gorn, lost touch with his family when he moved to Australian waters around 1870. He died in Adelaide in distraught circumstances in 1909.

• Hugh Linklater, engineer with the British India Steam Navigation Company, died in Calcutta in 1914 aged 38.

• Captain George Mowat of the *King David* died in the River Plate in 1925 aged 46.

• Father's cousin William Ritch died on Kaye & Company's S.S. *Marylyn* in Bristol in 1958 aged 49.

• Captain Sammy Ritch (son of Captain Magnus) became unfit for service after he was severely beaten up in America where he was salvaging gold bullion from a wreck in the Gulf of Mexico. He retired to London where he died in 1966 aged only 52.

• Captain Charlie Davidson survived the North Atlantic convoys of World War II and went on to work in the Persian Gulf where he had a fatal fall from the boarding ladder of a tanker in 1970, aged 50.

Charlie as an apprentice with the King Line
c. 1938

www.ingramcontent.com/pod-product-compliance
Lightning Source LLC
Chambersburg PA
CBHW061232070526
44584CB00030B/4085